CELEBRITY LIFE LAUNDRY

CELEBRITY LIFE LAUNDRY

By *This Morning's* Anjula Mutanda
and Ashley Pearson

JOHN BLAKE

Published by John Blake Publishing Ltd,
3 Bramber Court, 2 Bramber Road,
London W14 9PB, England

www.blake.co.uk

First published in paperback in 2007

ISBN: 978-1-84454-334-2

All rights reserved. No part of this publication may be reproduced, stored in a retrieval system, or in any form or by any means, without the prior permission in writing of the publisher, nor be otherwise circulated in any form of binding or cover other than that in which it is published and without a similar condition including this condition being imposed on the subsequent publisher.

British Library Cataloguing-in-Publication Data:

A catalogue record for this book is available from the British Library.

Design by www.envydesign.co.uk

Printed and bound in Great Britain by William Clowes Ltd, Beccles, Suffolk

1 3 5 7 9 10 8 6 4 2

© Text copyright Anjula Mutanda and Ashley Pearson 2007

Papers used by John Blake Publishing are natural, recyclable products made from wood grown in sustainable forests. The manufacturing processes conform to the environmental regulations of the country of origin.

Every attempt has been made to contact the relevant copyright-holders, but some were unobtainable. We would be grateful if the appropriate people could contact us.

Contents

	Introduction	xi
1	The Perfectionist	1
2	The Serial Romantic	35
3	The Thrill Seeker	69
4	The Natural Talent	103
5	The High Flyer	133
6	The Exhibitionist	165
7	The Flamboyant Performer	197
8	Love matters. Who's your perfect type – and who to steer clear of!	233
9	Resources for a little extra help	257
	Bibliography	265

Acknowledgements

Anjula Mutanda:
To my wonderful husband Roy. Thank-you for reading and re-reading the manuscript, giving invaluable advice, and showing incredible patience and encouragement. To my amazing and beautiful daughter Anoushka for your enthusiasm, love and ideas for the book title! To Ken, my father-in-law, who in life was the embodiment of wisdom, strength, and great humanity. And to my family, for always being there.

Thank-you also to Maggie Smith for your words of wisdom, love and patience in reading the text. A big thank you to Julia, Jo, Nicola, Dawn, Jonny and all at NCI for believing in the book, and for your unstinting support, encouragement and advice.

Thank-you Geraldine for all your positive energy.

Thanks to all my friends and colleagues at *This Morning* who listened to my idea for the book with encouragement, and soothed away my stress during the ups and downs. To Phillip and Fern for always being gorgeous, positive and supportive about the book. A special thanks to you, Shu, for taking the time to read the sample chapters and giving fantastic feedback.

To my darling Anya who truly supported me through my illness.

And finally to my writing partner and friend, Ashley. Thank you for your brilliance and inspiration.

Ashley Pearson:
To my friend Geraldine Woods, the most amazing, wise and supportive agent a girl could ask for – thank you for being my champion. To the wonderful Jon Roseman, thank you for taking this enthusiastic girl from NYC and dropping her smack in the middle of London – there is no one I'd rather have on my side in a fight. Thanks to the team at *This Morning,* for your continued love and support. Phillip and Fern, you are the nicest celebrities I've ever met, and without question the best in the business. To Richard Desmond and Paul Ashford, thank you for believing in me and helping me to get here.

Thank you also to Jeannette Walls for first spotting my instincts for gossip and giving me a standard to strive for. Huge thanks to Robin Stringer, for your constant encouragement as I tackled this project, as well as loaning me your impressive and brilliant writing skills. Thanks also to Mary Ann Lackland for your unwavering support: I treasure our friendship. Anthony Dorkants, Belinda Wanis and Margarita Jijina; your friendship and advice were greatly appreciated. Heather Pearson, your beauty and brilliance never ceases to astound me; I am so grateful for you and incredibly proud to be your sister.

CELEBRITY LIFE LAUNDRY

Thanks to my dad Gene Pearson for teaching me that nothing is impossible and to 'dream big'. And to my mother Sandra, this book is dedicated to you. Your strength, determination, generosity and infinite ability to love inspire all that I do. The truth is, I want to grow up to be just like you.

And finally, Anjula Mutanda, thank you for being my brilliant co-author and friend. I wouldn't have wanted to do this with anyone but you.

Anjula and Ashley would also like to thank our agent and lawyer Ian Bloom, for being there when we really needed you. To John Blake and the team at Blakes for having the vision to publish our book, and to Mark our editor, for patiently looking after us. We are deeply grateful.

Introduction

Celebrity Life Laundry goes where no self-help book has gone before. It delves into the lives of the world's most recognisable people – the much-admired A-list celebrities – to help you to understand the secrets of success in love and life. It offers you the opportunity to clear up the emotional untidiness weighing down your life by following the examples of people just like you who have made it to the top.

Celebrities such as Madonna live glamorous lives, but they have problems just as we do. And, love them or hate them, most of us know more about celebrities than we care to admit. We know that Tom Cruise used to be married to Nicole Kidman, that Brad Pitt and Angelina Jolie fell in love while filming *Mr and Mrs Smith* and that Victoria Beckham sheds her pregnancy weight at record speed. *Celebrity Life Laundry* shows you how to take all this 'trivial' information and use it to clean up the emotional rubbish and complicated clutter that is weighing you down. We get behind the headlines, and offer insights into what drives, motivates and inspires your favourite celebrities.

CELEBRITY LIFE LAUNDRY

And, by understanding them better, you can learn how to improve your own life.

Celebrity Life Laundry provides four unique ways to help you create the life you want:

1. *By analysing celebrities' lifestyles and seeing how they tackle their problems, you can compare your own experiences and see what you're doing right and where you may be going wrong.*
2. *By examining your past and your ways of thinking, you'll discover how your feelings and behaviour have developed.*
3. *By practising positive, effective techniques, you can learn to overcome self-defeating attitudes that have stopped you realising your full potential.*
4. *And by developing greater self-awareness, you can find out which relationships to steer clear of, and which ones work best for you.*

Your ultimate goal? To establish balance in your life.

Celebrity Life Laundry is not a book that will turn you into someone you're not. What it will do, however, is help you make the most of who you are, and empower you to make the necessary changes to achieve your goals and get everything correctly proportioned and balanced. That's important, because balanced people are aware of their strengths and weaknesses and can use that knowledge to help themselves fulfil their potential.

CELEBRITY LIFE LAUNDRY
GETTING BEHIND THE HEADLINES

It's actually helpful to the rest of us that celebrities go public about their problems. As we see them overcome a run of bad relationships, or a problem childhood, and manage to get help and succeed, we realise that maybe we can too. Princess Diana blew the cover off bulimia, and allowed women who had experienced similar anguish to seek help. The actress and writer Carrie Fisher helped thousands when she admitted to suffering from manic depression, and shared her methods of dealing with it. Kylie Minogue went public about her battle with breast cancer, prompting thousands of young women to get medical check-ups.

And look how Jennifer Aniston handled her break-up with Brad Pitt. Losing her husband and watching him pair up with a gorgeous girl six years her junior must have been devastating. So what was Jen's reaction? Did she just decide she was not good enough, not worthy of love? Did she just sit at home in her pyjamas eating Big Macs? No – she invested time and energy in taking care of herself. First, she embarked on a new exercise regime that included martial arts (to get rid of her rage) and yoga to help her relax. Then she threw herself into making three films back-to-back, keeping herself busy so she couldn't sit around moping. And she started dating again. Months after the split from Brad, she and new boyfriend Vince Vaughn could be seen out enjoying themselves in bars and comedy clubs. Jen said she'd danced more in the months since her break-up than she did in the seven years she was with Brad.

The A-listers are shaped and affected just as we are by

experiences in our early childhood, feelings of insecurity, low self-esteem and relationship problems. As Goldie Hawn once said, 'There isn't anyone in show business who doesn't want to be loved, and it usually comes from some deficit in childhood.'

THE SEVEN PERSONALITY TYPES

This book describes seven key personality types, based on common psychological characteristics that reflect different mental approaches, and uses celebrity examples as illustrations. From the outlines we provide, you should then be able to identify your own personality type, so you'll be better able to understand not just what makes the balanced celebrities tick, but what makes you tick too. Each chapter covers one of the seven types:

Chapter 1 tackles the Perfectionist – Madonna, Russell Crowe and Victoria Beckham.
Chapter 2 covers the Serial Romantic – Jennifer Lopez, Julia Roberts and Brad Pitt.
Chapter 3 investigates the Thrill Seeker – Kate Moss, Angelina Jolie and Tom Cruise.
Chapter 4 looks at the Natural Talent – Nicole Kidman, Robbie Williams and Jennifer Aniston.
Chapter 5 examines the High Flyer – Oprah Winfrey, Catherine Zeta Jones and Sarah Jessica Parker.
Chapter 6 is devoted to the Exhibitionist – Pamela Anderson, Jordan and Paris Hilton.
Chapter 7 studies the Flamboyant Performer –

CELEBRITY LIFE LAUNDRY

Sharon Stone, Sharon Osbourne and Elton John. Chapter 8 examines which of these character types might be your best hope for long-lasting love – and which type to avoid!

And Chapter 9 offers a little extra help, with a list of organisations and groups from which the reader can get further help on more serious, deep-rooted issues.

Think about how you react to a specific event. Everyone does it differently. While failure might leave the extreme Perfectionist feeling anxious and out of control, the High Flyer might be completely undeterred, eager to try again. If you are a Perfectionist like Madonna, you are probably too hard on yourself and others; if you thirst for thrills like Angelina Jolie, you may have trouble sustaining relationships. If your ex was a Serial Romantic like Brad Pitt, you may find it impossible to get over him; and if you are plagued by self-doubt, you may have more in common with Nicole Kidman, the Natural Talent, than you could have imagined.

You may also discover that you fit into more than one category – most of the celebrities do too. But, while people are often a combination of types, one type usually dominates and shapes the way they operate. We have therefore categorised the celebrities in this book according to their dominant positive behavioural characteristics. Which type are you?

CELEBRITY LIFE LAUNDRY
SOLUTIONS

Getting to know yourself better

A healthy level of self-awareness is an essential ingredient for private and public success. By increasing your self-awareness, you'll become alert to how you think, feel and behave. Otherwise, you may become blind to what is going on around you and remain stuck forever in a cycle of constantly repeating negative behavioural patterns.

So the first question is: what makes us the way we are?

We are all influenced by a complex combination of factors – our genes, family and friends, and the environment – and they help shape our personalities. How much each factor contributes is difficult to quantify. However, we all end up with a 'script' – i.e. how we see ourselves, and the way we think and feel about who we are. The bad news is that if we stick to these restrictive scripts of who we are, we might become trapped by our histories and confined by negative beliefs. And though we may want to change our lives, there's a chance we might be too frightened to let go of tried-and-tested strategies. That's because, while these strategies might not make us happy, they do at least make us feel safe, since their outcome is largely predictable.

The good news is that, by recognising how our experiences, and other factors, have influenced us both positively and negatively, we can decide to change how we think. We can break repeated patterns that hurt us, shrug off unhealthy labels such as 'not good enough' or 'failure', learn to lead more positive lives and end up by fulfilling our potential.

Therefore, the aim of examining each of the personality types is to move from behaviour that is both negative and harmful to the individual – described in this book as being an 'extreme' of the personality type – to working towards balanced behaviour that is more constructive, positive and self-aware.

Cognitive Behavioural Therapy

Although there about 450 types of therapy, there is a large body of scientific evidence to support the effectiveness of Cognitive Behavioural Therapy (CBT) when tackling a wide range of problems from depression, low self-esteem and anxiety to relationship difficulties. The National Institute for Clinical Excellence (NICE) endorses CBT as its therapy of choice when treating depression and anxiety. That's why in *Celebrity Life Laundry* we explain and use CBT techniques and skills. They could help you change your thinking and improve your life.

WHAT IS CBT?

Cognitive Behavioural Therapy is really a combination of two kinds of therapy.

The cognitive side helps you to examine how certain types of thinking can lead to a distorted picture of what may be going on in your life. This in turn can have a knock-on effect on how you feel – perhaps leading to you becoming anxious, distressed or angry, for instance.

The behavioural side helps you to challenge and then change your habitual behaviours and distorted beliefs.

CELEBRITY LIFE LAUNDRY
CBT EXPLAINED

Imagine the following situation.

> A (activating event): A friend doesn't acknowledge you in the supermarket.
>
> B (extreme belief): 'My friend froze me out. That means she is upset with me. It's dreadful when people don't like me.'
>
> C (emotional and behavioural consequence): You feel anxious, and go out of your way to avoid your friend.

By looking at this sequence of events in terms of three steps – ABC – you can see how a number of assumptions are made along the way:

You've been frozen out.

Your friend is upset with you.

People don't like you.

What you have here is a set of negative assumptions and a 'catastrophising' of the event. A more reasonable and rational explanation could be that your friend didn't see you because her mind was on other things. Your friend may go out of her way to ignore everyone when she is in a foul mood, so, even if she did ignore you, it does not mean that she is upset with you, or that people don't like you.

A better response would be: 'My friend didn't see me in the supermarket maybe because she had things on her mind and didn't notice me. I'll give her a call later, and see how she is.'

By reframing your thinking, you feel less anxious, behave

in a more rational way and are not ruled by negative beliefs about yourself.

Writing it down
Throughout the book, we suggest when it might be helpful to keep a diary, writing down and assessing your thoughts so that you can instantly spot any irrational beliefs. By using the ABC model in each chapter, you will be able to see examples of how thoughts, feelings and actions can lead to negative beliefs about yourself. They may include states of all-or-nothing, learned helplessness and over-generalised thinking. Such irrational ways of thinking can lead to distress and negative outcomes. Through a series of self-help exercises, you will also learn how to challenge and then change your attitudes in order to eliminate the negatives and become positive, so that you're back in control.

Loving better
No self-help book would be complete without advice on how to make your romantic relationships more fulfilling. At the end of every chapter, there is a section on relationships, which will help you to:

> Take a closer look at the choices you make when it comes to love.
> Examine how your style of thinking propels you into choosing certain kinds of people.
> Increase your awareness, so that you can make more informed and better choices about whom you date.

CELEBRITY LIFE LAUNDRY

A-list celebrities possess some of life's most desirable personality traits, including determination, persistence and the will to overcome astronomical odds. *Celebrity Life Laundry* makes it possible for you to understand yourself better, change your way of thinking, and find balance as you negotiate your way towards success in life and love. All that will be left for you to do is to fulfill your dreams – just like they have.

1
The Perfectionist

Being a Perfectionist sounds like an ideal gold standard, doesn't it? You push yourself to the limit and aim for being the best at whatever you do. Life is all about being a winner. But is this a healthy pursuit of excellence, or just a big stick with which to hit yourself?

There are many definitions of a Perfectionist, but there are five common characteristics on which psychologists agree:

1. The goal of the Perfectionist is to set, and focus on, unrealistically high standards.
2. The Perfectionist doesn't feel satisfied with anything that's less than perfect.
3. The Perfectionist is preoccupied with fear of failure.
4. The Perfectionist engages in all-or-nothing thinking.
5. The Perfectionist views making mistakes as proof that he or she is not good enough.

THE PERFECTIONIST

In the article 'Perfectionism and Underachievement', the psychologist M. Adderholt-Elliot also identified the 'paralysed Perfectionist', with reference to those who are so fearful of getting something wrong that they do nothing instead. Gordon Flett, a psychologist who specialises in research on Perfectionist thinking, identified three types of Perfectionist who vary in their approach. They are:

1. The Perfectionist who demands perfection in others.
2. The Perfectionist who thinks that others expect perfection from them.
3. The Perfectionist who demands perfection from themselves.

Research also suggests that certain forms of Perfectionist behaviour can be linked to a whole host of physical, relationship and emotional problems, including depression, anorexia, bulimia and migraines.

Being a balanced Perfectionist is the ideal, encompassing the ability to use one's strengths positively, while also understanding where one's vulnerabilities lie. The ability to stay focused, achieve goals and aim to be the best are just some of the balanced Perfectionist's attributes. Difficulties occur, however, when the individual gets out of balance and becomes an extreme Perfectionist.

So let's get back to our celebrities. Based on what we know about them, what dominant features of a balanced Perfectionist do the following have?

CELEBRITY LIFE LAUNDRY

MADONNA – THE DRIVEN PERFECTIONIST

'I've lost track of how many times I've been written off. Maybe that's the reason I cried when I heard about the record. Here's a big scoop. We're human, too.' Madonna

As Madonna headed to the stage during her summer 2006 Confessions tour, everything seemed very much 'business as usual'. While other artists such as Pink stop to chat and hug their crew before showtime, Madonna is known for treating this walk to the stage like a journey to the office – it's her job, and she's serious about it. But this concert was different. Just before the sweaty June songfest in California's San José, the Queen of pop made a trip backstage in her trademark designer tracksuit to say hello to the video crew. 'She said "Hi" to everybody and "Have a good show." We were all quite shocked,' said Madge's sound engineer Jason Harvey, who explained that the megastar tends to keep to herself. 'It was lovely to hear. The lady is a perfectionist,' he continues. 'She works 110 per cent, and that's what she expects from all of her people.'

Madonna herself told the *New York Post* in June 2006, 'I have to be satisfied with what I do. Not that I ever am. I mean, I'm always thinking something can be done better. But, I absolutely appreciate commercial success and it means so much if my fans, who have been devoted through thick and thin, like what I do. When this album debuted at No. 1, when it was No. 1 around the world at the same time, I opened up a bottle of champagne and I cried.'

THE PERFECTIONIST

Madonna's perfectionism is legendary. And she is harder on no one than she is on herself. When the superstar was thrown from the saddle of her horse on her 47th birthday, she calmly stood up, walked across the grounds of her £10-million Wiltshire mansion and got herself to hospital. She gritted her teeth in an emergency room while she was treated for a broken collarbone, three cracked ribs and a shattered hand. In spite of her injuries, and within days of her fall, she attended the premiere of her husband Guy's new film, clad in a black sequinned dress, thigh-high boots and a designer sling. Within weeks, she appeared on television programmes around the world to promote her new record, decked out as a 1970s dance queen with feather-cut hair. And she even created a special dance routine for the recording of her new video to allow for her damaged collarbone, telling one reporter, 'My left arm is flapping around like a chicken wing and I don't have any strength right now. I'm going to invent some new dance move that doesn't use the bad bits. I'm still a tough girl.'

Madonna has made millions as a singing superstar and international icon, but she still shows no sign of letting up. Now approaching the age of 50, she is determined to prove that she can still do it all. An active mother with two children – Lourdes and Rocco – she has learned to ride horses, shoot game and become the perfect country gentlewoman for her English husband.

Madonna has also turned her Perfectionist eye on her figure. The one-time Material Girl is built like a well-oiled machine, a product of years of carefully thought-out planning. Her passion for yoga is legendary, and her strict macrobiotic eating regime has converted fellow celebrities such as Gwyneth Paltrow. She is said to exercise for a staggering five hours every day, and, as Madonna has evolved, so have her workouts. In the 1980s, she ran ten miles a day and spent hours lifting weights. When she became pregnant with Lourdes, she didn't let it slow her down; she did 45 minutes on a Stairmaster seven days a week. Pilates came next, which led to her passion for the more vigorous Ashtanga yoga. Madonna practises Ashtanga in her home gym for two hours each morning, and has become one of the most advanced Ashtanga yogis in Britain. She also jogs, pumps iron and swims. She even uses a wooden rack to stretch and tone her already taut muscles, using a technique called 'gyro tonic expansion'.

Her hard work has paid off: Madonna sports the kind of biceps any athlete would be proud of. In the video for her hit single 'Hung Up', her body is more like that of a pre-adolescent girl than a 47-year-old mother of two. To the outside observer, however, it might seem as though Madonna has been physically punishing herself for more than two decades. She herself once admitted, 'That is why I work so hard. I work at not being self-destructive. My nature is to fight back – to fight those demons.'

Born into a large lower-middle-class Italian-American family in Bay City, Michigan, in 1958, the childhood of Madonna Louise Veronica Ciccone was marked by a major milestone: her mother's death. This loss, when Madonna was just five years old, was the single most

THE PERFECTIONIST

During her Confessions tour, Madonna reportedly shouted at an audience member at her gig in Las Vegas, Nevada, in May 2006 when she noticed that he wasn't dancing to her disco hits. Madonna startled her audience when, midway through the concert, she stopped singing and singled out a man in the front row, who wasn't getting into the groove. 'If you are only going to sit there, at least you can smile,' she yelled at him.

Tickets for a Madonna concert are like gold dust, with fans expecting nothing short of a life-changing experience. Her 120-date Drowned World tour sold out immediately and earned around $120 million, with an attendance around the 920,000 mark. But there's a price to pay for her level of performance. Madonna has called her life 'exhausting. There isn't a second in my day that isn't taken up looking after my family or thinking about my show.'

The pop superstar has enjoyed a long and incredibly successful career, but she insists that each new achievement touches her heart. She told the *New York Post*, 'It was my husband, Guy, who told me the album was number one in America. I was shocked, stunned, happy. I said, "We have to celebrate." So we opened a bottle of champagne – not something I usually do, though I probably should do more of that – I had a glass, and then I sat and cried for 20 minutes. Really. So many conflicting emotions, but basically tears of joy. Don't let anybody tell you commercial success doesn't matter.'

defining moment of her early years. The daughter of a strict Catholic father, she sought acceptance and approval in other places. As an adolescent, she practised dancing for hours a day, and left home for the bright lights of New York as soon as she could. In the song 'Mer Girl' from the *Ray of Light* album, Madonna sings about this traumatising loss, ending with the lyrics: 'And I smelled her burning flesh/Her rotting bones/Her decay/And I ran and I ran/I'm still running today.'

Some 40 years on, Perfectionist Madonna still seeks her dad's approval. The superstar shocked audiences night after night during her recent Confessions tour, by shouting out the f-word, reaching inside her pants, and flipping her middle finger at the audience. But at one show in Chicago, a very different Madonna emerged – it seemed her father was in the sold-out crowd. 'She gave the crowd the finger only one time and never once said the f-word,' recalled a concert-goer at that show. 'At one point, she actually asked the audience to applaud extra loud for her so that her dad would know she made something of herself. The crowd went wild.'

In the last few years, Madonna's perfectionism has also extended to spiritual matters. As an ardent follower of Kabbalah, she has banished swearing and virtually all television from her life and that of her family. This is a seismic shift for a woman who became notorious by posing naked in orgiastic scenes for her *Sex* book. Today, spiritual beliefs are as much a part of Madonna's life as her cone-shaped bras and sexual independence were in the 1980s. She doesn't gossip, keeps her ego in check and

THE PERFECTIONIST

has asked friends to refer to her simply as 'M'. There is Madonna the star and the businesswoman, who astutely understands that controversy can attract attention and secure column inches. But there is also Madonna the mother, who wants to move away from that edgy approach and to steer her own children down a quieter, more mature road.

Her performance on stage is certainly a testament to her Perfectionist nature. During her Drowned World tour, Madonna spent up to eight hours a day rehearsing. 'I feel very blessed. I can't complain,' a weary Madonna admitted to reporters before her five-night sold-out stint in New York. During one song, the consummate performer stunned fans when she flew *Crouching Tiger, Hidden Dragon*-style above a 4,900sq-ft stage, before landing gracefully. It wasn't as easy as it looked. She was rumoured to have spent two hours a day a month beforehand, tirelessly practising how to leap and twirl while dangling from a harness on a rig.

What's more, Madonna seems to have turned her eye for perfection towards her home life too. Amid published reports of cracks in her marriage to Guy Ritchie, the star admitted, 'It's not easy having a good marriage, but I don't want easy. I thank God every day that I married a man who made me think. That's my definition of true love.' In a 2006 interview with *Elle* magazine, Madonna claimed she would like to allow herself a few more curves, but revealed that she kept herself slim for Guy. 'I wish I were comfortable enough to look *zaftig*,' she said, using a Yiddish phrase meaning pleasingly plump. 'But I choose men who like carved-out women, the "Can you run for the bus?" kind of guy.'

It is clear that, regardless of the outcome of her marriage to Guy, Madonna will survive. Her chief talent is the ability to reinvent herself in ways that have shocked and delighted millions of fans. Asked why he admires his idol, one fan replied, 'Madonna's a pioneer. Most pop stars today are anorexic, drugged out or are dangling their kids out of windows. She knows how to take a fall and get back up.'

Analyse this: Madonna

Madonna seems to exhibit many of the classic signs of a Perfectionist thinker. Being the best seems to be her mantra and she is driven to achieve in every area she puts her mind to.

At the tender age of five, the point at which children start school and naturally start moving away from parental security, Madonna suffered a huge personal loss with the death of her mother. This might well have left its own emotional imprint and traumatic scar on her. It is the point at which a child begins to understand the permanency of death.

As the middle child, Madonna may have fought for attention and felt driven to stand out from her siblings. Research on middle children reflects that they often feel they have to work harder to get noticed, or be heard by their parents. Her father remarried very quickly, and Madonna and her siblings had no choice in the matter. This could have also had a negative psychological impact. Like

THE PERFECTIONIST

any other child, Madonna may have at first rebelled against this new and alien influence in her world; she may have struggled with angry feelings that her own mother was being replaced by someone she did not want in her life.

Madonna's emotional relationship with her father has been well documented over the years. However, a key theme that appears over and over again is her desire to win his approval. Madonna's father himself says that he used to reward her for her achievements, and he describes the young Madonna as an achiever. Perhaps this was part of what shaped who she is today. Her identity may have become wrapped up in what she achieved and not simply who she was as a person – so much so that it seems as though, even to this day, her father still remains the one person Madonna still aims to truly impress. Perhaps she feels that this unconditional praise still eludes her. It therefore comes as no surprise that Madonna revealed in an interview in 2005 – with TV station Channel 4 – that, to understand her, people had to know her dad.

Madonna has regularly reinvented herself – to appeal to a new generation of fans, to win their approval. With this level of determination and success, there seems to be little room for enjoyment and relaxation in what she has achieved, as there is always another goal round the corner – a characteristically Perfectionist approach.

There is no doubt that she is motivated, focused, driven by a desire for self-improvement and constantly searching out ways of being the best she can. As she has grown older, become a mother and remarried, her energies have changed from drawing attention to herself and not caring whether it was positive or negative to wanting to discover a more balanced way of being.

Interestingly, at times Madonna appears to contradict herself by banning profanity and then swearing like a trooper when on tour. Perhaps this is indicative of a tension between two contrary impulses in the singer. Madonna may always struggle to keep her Perfectionist thinking in check, as exemplified by her horse-riding accident. Instead of allowing herself time to rest, recover and heal, she was back working within days. She didn't allow herself to be anything but in control, and aimed to meet her own very high standards. But, by channelling her efforts in ways that are more meaningful to her – whether this means her family, Kabbalah, or yoga – she may also have enabled herself to use her Perfectionist energy in a more balanced and positive way.

RUSSELL CROWE – THE ANGRY PERFECTIONIST

'I'm obviously a complicated, messy, psychologically damaged weirdo, and that's the fundamental requirement for my job. It's unfortunate that people don't just understand that and leave me to my padded cell.' Russell Crowe

Russell Crowe has wanted to share the big screen with long-time friend and colleague Nicole Kidman for more than a decade. Therefore, it must have given him great satisfaction when he was chosen to play the Aussie

THE PERFECTIONIST

actress's lover in a film set around the Japanese bombing of Australia in 1942. The $150-million epic would be directed by fellow Aussie Baz Lurham. It was a dream come true – but it was not to last. Before long, Crowe was dumped from the film in favour of Hugh Jackman. It was widely reported that the film's producers had dropped him after the star demanded full script approval. Russell denied this and expressed surprise at his removal from the project, commenting, 'My reps stand by their efforts in trying to make this work... we did not disengage, Baz and Fox did.'

Whatever the truth behind the sudden change of leading man, it was the latest in a long line of stories about the difficult genius that is Russell Crowe.

When Russell Crowe reportedly hurled a phone at a New York hotel employee just after 4am in early June 2005, it was simply regarded as one more outburst from a man who has become famous for his temper as well as his talent. There was that brawl in a Sydney nightclub in which he was filmed kicking a bouncer, followed by reports that he'd slammed a BAFTA producer against a wall for cutting short Crowe's poetic acceptance speech. He has been called arrogant, surly and grouchy, and he is one of Hollywood's loudest Perfectionists.

Russell was born in New Zealand. His family later moved to Australia, where his parents managed pubs and later had a catering business, which meant they often worked on television and film sets. The actor has admitted that there was never financial stability in his early life. 'I didn't want to be a dad under those circumstances,' he admitted, years later. 'I never wanted to have children who would hear the kind of conversations I had to hear my parents having, wondering where the money was going to come from for the next rent.'

His home life was boisterous, to say the least. 'I grew up in a competitive household, and my brother is 16 months older than me. If you didn't speak loudest, you simply weren't heard.' He claims that he is actually a gentle man, 'But I also have grown up in this society where if you show gentleness you're a poof.'

Russell burst on to the scene with his brilliant performance in 1997's *LA Confidential*, and in 2000 he won the Academy Award for his role in *Gladiator*. Before long, he had become universally recognised as one of Hollywood's greatest and most dedicated leading men. Director Michael Mann says he knew immediately that he wanted Russell to play the paunchy 53-year-old Jeffrey Wigand, the biochemist at the heart of *The Insider*. At the time Crowe was 34, fighting fit and had never even heard of Wigand, but sources say he won the part in a single reading. According to Mann, 'He was truly "in the moment". In one line of dialogue, I saw Jeffrey Wigand there.'

To prepare for the role, the Aussie actor perfected his American accent, put on 50 pounds and dyed his hair seven times. He felt he still didn't look old enough, however, so he shaved his head for a wig. By the time filming started, Crowe simply *was* Wigand, with folds of fat around his face and an improvised waddle.

THE PERFECTIONIST

But such dedication comes at a price. When Russell began working with Australian director Peter Weir on the epic *Master and Commander*, he warned, 'At some stage during the movie, you will see me get really upset with myself. Do not get involved in that maelstrom because it's got nothing to do with you, I'll sort it out.'

> The Museum of the Moving Image tribute to Ron Howard turned into something of a roast of Russell Crowe – maybe because the phone-throwing actor wasn't around to kick butts, the *New York Daily News* reports. Jim Carrey introduced a clip from the Howard-directed *The Grinch* by observing, 'A lot of people don't think Ron is tough. But he's done a couple of movies with Russell Crowe and there isn't a mark on him.' Then again, Carrey added, 'I haven't seen him with his shirt off lately.'
>
> In *Cinderella Man*, Russell Crowe plays boxer James Braddock, a successful 1930s prizefighter. He spent long days in the gym and extended sessions with stunt co-ordinators and boxing experts to ensure the fight scenes in the movie were realistic. Crowe was prepared to put the time in; he says others were not. Actor Craig Bierko was cast to play Braddock's rival, Max Baer. In an interview with the *LA Times*, Bierko said that Crowe barely spoke to him during the project despite many hours together on set. 'He had his 40th birthday party and I was the one guy who wasn't invited,' Bierko said.
>
> When Crowe met reporters in New York after

> Bierko's words were printed, he was not happy. His complaint was that he believed Bierko arrived on set unprepared. 'When Craig arrived in Toronto, he realised he was probably further behind than what he should be,' Crowe said dismissively.
>
> A disappointed Crowe raised the issue with director Ron Howard and Bierko's 'workload got significantly heavier in Toronto'. 'Craig has an incredibly vibrant sense of humour but that was just not suitable for this gig,' Crowe revealed. 'He tends to have this ability to talk to the person who is training him into the belief "We've done a lot of work today". I saw him do that to three different trainers, so I brought in somebody that he wouldn't be able to do it to.'
>
> Russell Crowe has a request for his fans – stop giving his wife Danielle Spencer sympathetic looks. After his arrest for throwing a phone at a NYC hotel employee, the Oscar-winning star says that the public seem to think his singer/actress wife Spencer is a saint for putting up with her husband's unpredictability. Crowe says, 'My wife is heartily sick of the dour-faced, sad-eyed looks that people give her on the street and she sometimes wishes she could take every one of those people aside and tell them how fabulous her life is.'

His commitment was admirable. For the shipboard epic, Russell fought off chronic seasickness, conquered his fear of heights to climb a ship's mast, and nearly drowned during a storm sequence. And, although it was

THE PERFECTIONIST

not necessary, Crowe learned to play the violin for just one scene. It wasn't easy. According to Russell, 'She's a very harsh mistress, the violin. Nothing has been more difficult than learning to play the violin – not tiger fights, helicopter stunts or gunfights. But I made a pact with myself that I wouldn't pretend. So I practised for 18 to 25 hours a week and had three different teachers.'

Crowe's director on *Gladiator*, Ridley Scott, said that the star was a challenge to work with, but added, 'Russell is worth it.'

According to Russell's director and friend Ron Howard, the actor is like a force of nature – and not always a co-operative one. 'Directing Russell is like shooting on a tropical island,' Howard admits. 'The weather is going to change several times a day, but you're shooting there for a reason. Sometimes those dark clouds are just what you need. And sometimes you wish it would stop raining so you can do the sunny scene.'

In a September 2005 interview, Russell declared that he hates being called a 'knockabout bloke' because it implies that he's someone who doesn't care, who isn't engaged and disciplined. 'Do you have any idea the level of personal control that I have, to get to where I am? Any idea at all? This thing of being a smoking gun, this lit fuse, it's just bollocks,' he says. 'Vincit qui se vincit.' ('He conquers who conquers himself.')

Analyse this: Russell Crowe

In preparation for *Cinderella Man*, Crowe gave up drinking to lose 49 pounds. This is only the most recent instance of the actor's intense, sometimes volatile compulsion to accept no limits in the characters he is playing, and the lengths to which he will go to become the consummate actor. Although at times he is undone by his temper, Crowe's conscious objective is an unparalleled level of excellence, and the end result is a mix of rave reviews and the lack of any real popularity in Hollywood. Crowe clearly illustrates the way that being a Perfectionist thinker can be a double-edged sword.

It's clear that Russell Crowe could never quite fit in. Certainly not when growing up in Australia. 'You have to be a bloke if you want to live in Australia, but I'm not really a bloke, you know?' he once revealed. 'I didn't grow up the high-school jock. I'm a very interior person. These roles I've played that have a kind of physical element to them, they're all great achievements because I never really was a very physical person.'

The real Russell, the lad one primary-school teacher called 'a lovely, sensitive little boy', is closer to the tortured mathematician John Nash in *A Beautiful Mind* than to the Coliseum avenger Maximus Decimus Meridius.

We have seen that, by his own admission, Crowe grew up in a competitive household. This would perhaps have marked the beginning of him wanting to be the best, outdoing his sibling and jostling for position to gain attention and praise. Research on same-sex siblings with a small age gap certainly bears out the competitive nature of the rivalry between Crowe and his older brother, and the struggle to be the victor.

THE PERFECTIONIST

In his pursuit of perfectionism, however, Russell appears to be paying the price. The Perfectionist's attitude – second best isn't good enough – leads to troubled relationships, because it doesn't allow for the needs of others. In Crowe's case, this process works itself out on his film sets. In his quest to be perfect, Russell appears to strive compulsively to stay in control of what he is doing, taking criticism as a personal attack and, as a result, frustrating those with whom he works. This is a powerful irony, because one of the things that Perfectionists really crave is to be loved and accepted.

Russell also appears to have worked very hard to develop a macho outer layer – perhaps to mask his vulnerability, and as a means of survival. A sad consequence may be that he feels isolated from those around him. However, there is no doubt that he is driven and ambitious, and when these qualities are in balance they can lead to great achievements, as Russell has shown in his career.

VICTORIA BECKHAM – PICTURE-PERFECT PERFECTIONIST

It was months in the planning and cost £500,000. Dubbed 'Full Length and Fabulous', Victoria Beckham's pre-World Cup charity bash looked set to be the event of the year. Guests included Australian supermodel Elle Macpherson, who arrived with fashionable property developer John Hitchcox. The Duchess of York and daughter Princess Beatrice also made it. Among the other guests were rap mogul P Diddy, former Spice Girls Emma Bunton and Melanie Brown, Christian Slater, Sharon and Ozzy Osbourne, Jerry Hall and Nick Faldo. England team stars including Wayne Rooney, Michael Owen, Ashley Cole, Gary Neville, Frank Lampard, John Terry and Paul Robinson were also there.

But despite careful planning and extravagant touches – food prepared by celebrated chef Gordon Ramsay, decorative trees flown in from Spain – little went according to plan. A fly-over of Battle of Britain planes was cancelled after angry protests and, just when it seemed things couldn't get any worse, the heavens opened, putting an end to the planned fireworks display. As the night fell apart, Victoria was reported to have flown into a screaming fit. One observer said she was berating organisers 'like a lunatic'. And yet, if you had been one of the many thousands who bought *Hello!* magazine one week later, you would have been treated to a front-page shot of Victoria, resplendent in her Roberto Cavalli gown slashed to the waist, dancing triumphantly on the dance floor – arm extended in unadulterated rapture – accompanied by a quote from her adoring husband, David: 'I'd like to thank my beautiful wife, who is a wonderful mother, for all her love and effort in putting on this party.' It was spin control at its finest.

And this was not the first time. Who could forget those memorable photos of Victoria just days after allegations emerged that David had had an affair with personal assistant Rebecca Loos. It was red-carpet posing to end all posing. Standing with an arched back, fixing a

THE PERFECTIONIST

sparkling grin, Victoria Beckham shot one coy look after another at the press, all the while tightly gripping her David's hand. Given the allegations on every front page in the country, Victoria's fixed smile and sexy poses in a tight designer dress as she clung to her husband left the tabloid press incredulous.

But perhaps the stress of such a public scandal – which the Beckhams have consistently insisted is completely without foundation – took its toll on the beautiful star. Widely recognised as a fashion clotheshorse, Victoria Beckham is regularly spotted wearing the latest in D&G, Roberto Cavalli and Louis Vuitton. And when she selected her wardrobe for the 2006 World Cup, Victoria knew the stakes were high – the eyes of the world would be on her. When the wife of the England captain hit the streets of Germany, she arrived with trunkfuls of the very latest in fashionable attire. The glamorous mum of three was regularly photographed wearing tiny denim hotpants with a skinny vest, while tottering around on skyscraper-high stilettos. But it was not her carefully chosen ensemble that made headlines – it was her stick-thin legs and emaciated frame. Headlines such as 'Is Posh Losing her Spice' and 'Not Posh to Be So Skinny' were trumpeted around the world; the universal consensus appeared to be that Victoria had gone too far in her quest to be thin. She was gaunt and rarely smiled for photographers. In her autobiography, Victoria Beckham came close to admitting that she had once struggled with an eating disorder. She denied being anorexic, 'but I was probably very close to it. I could tell you the fat and calorie content in absolutely anything.' And whatever diet she was currently following, judging from her tiny frame critics were quick to speculate that she had once again gone too far. She was a shadow of her former self.

It must be said that Victoria regularly looks picture perfect. For a spot of sightseeing with her husband in Paris, Victoria wore a micro-mini skirt and towering stiletto sandals. The sheer height of those heels would have made it impossible for most women to cross the street, let alone spend a day walking across the cobbled alleys of the City of Lights. While Hollywood stars such as Jennifer Aniston and Madonna are often photographed in tracksuits or scruffy jeans with ratty hair and clutching a Starbucks coffee, Victoria always looks camera ready.

After giving birth to her son Cruz, Victoria didn't leave her house until she'd shed every single ounce of her baby weight. She seems to be so dedicated to the preservation of her flawless image as a wife and as an object of desire that she never goes out without full make-up, hair extensions, the chicest designer clothes and dripping in diamonds.

She is also committed to showing the world that her marriage is a happy one. David and Victoria recently sued and then settled with the *News of the World* over their story that the Beckham marriage was a sham. The paper had claimed that the marriage was an arrangement created to protect the duo's business interests, cynically dubbed 'Brand Beckham'. The couple claimed that they had been defamed and libelled – they insisted that their

THE PERFECTIONIST

marriage was real, and happy, and they wanted the world to know that.

Victoria's childhood was not a fairy tale. As a little girl, she was teased by her peers. She has admitted in interviews that, 'I've never had a lot of friends. Even when I was at school I was never popular.' Did it upset her? 'Yeah, everybody wants to have loads of friends.

> **While pregnant with baby son Cruz, Victoria Beckham reportedly piled on more than 2st. Uncomfortable with her size, and fed up with 'feeling fat', Victoria hid out in her Madrid mansion until she had ruthlessly dieted off all her extra weight in five weeks. That's a shocking loss of nearly 6 pounds per week! In order to make such a dramatic change, rumours abounded that Victoria had devised her own weight-loss plan that's stricter than the famous Atkins diet. In order to lose weight fast she is reported to have resorted to eating just a few types of food a week. She allegedly ate only various types of fish, salad leaves and bananas. And her tuna and cod were always grilled or steamed. Mrs Beckham drank two litres of water a day, as well as green tea and two glasses of milk. A source close to the ex-Spice Girl said, 'After a week Victoria allowed herself chicken, and other fruits such as strawberries as well as green vegetables. But that was it.'**
>
> **'She's determined to sort her flab out quickly,' husband David told the press.**

Maybe that's why I am like I am now,' she once confessed. At school, she had a bad acne problem and had her share of teasing and bullying. What's more, classmates didn't like the fact that sometimes her father picked her up from school in a Rolls-Royce. It caused her a lot of pain. 'I would wake up and worry about who I was going to sit next to in class,' she remembered. As an adult, she has learned to be wary of people; she does not trust them easily and has stated that she 'doesn't want any new friends'.

After the worldwide success of the Spice Girls, Victoria struggled with her solo career, and she was forced to deal with less-than-generous reviews of her singing. But she never gave up. She admits, 'I don't need to work like I did in the old days when I needed to earn a living. But I'm a complete perfectionist, so when I work on a song I never just leave. I could be in the studio till five, six and seven in the morning.'

Her love for David is fierce. This is the same woman who once told a soccer player, after hearing of his penchant for rough play, 'If you ever kick my husband I'll come round and kick you.' She is the one who protected Becks when he was demonised as the petulant boy who ruined England's chances in the 1998 World Cup. He ran straight into the arms of his famous then girlfriend. 'When I say I don't fancy anyone else and I don't look at them, that's because nobody is remotely attractive compared to David. I look at him and I idolise him. I would do anything for him,' she gushed.

Victoria was asked several years ago what she would

THE PERFECTIONIST

do if she found out that David was having an affair. After careful thought she responded, 'I think it'd kill me. I'd die of a broken heart. I know it sounds clichéd, but that would probably be what would happen; my career is important to me, but it's not what keeps me happy. If what keeps me happy was damaged it would kill me, it really would.' And when reports of David's alleged extramarital affair with Rebecca Loos did surface, Victoria defended her husband vehemently.

Victoria's perfectionism drives her to maintain her glamorous appearance at all times and to be as loving as possible. She works tirelessly at maintaining the perfect marriage, at being the dream wife to a man she keeps on a pedestal, and being a loving mother to her children. She seems consumed with doing it all right for David, and with the idea of being in a position of power – demonstrating that she has her life together so completely that no one is ever going to get one over on her.

Analyse this: Victoria Beckham

Victoria appears to have it all, materially speaking, and strives to keep the whole package ticking over perfectly. There seems to be a deep-rooted drive in her to be the very best she can in order to win love and approval. This may have been reinforced by being rejected by her peers at school, who effectively told her that she didn't belong with them. She may have countered this as a child by working very hard to hide her hurt feelings, and trying to fit in.

Victoria might believe that others expect nothing less

than perfection from her. So it may be that, no matter what is happening in her life, she feels unable to show her pain or reveal any flaws. This is evident in her appearance in front of the cameras, and her ability to smile through the excruciating pain of the reports that her husband had had an affair. The emotional effects of an affair are countless. There is anger, resentment, loss of trust and depression. Victoria's pain must have been immense, and yet her Perfectionist side could not betray her anguish.

Some researchers have made a connection between a Perfectionist mindset and suffering from eating disorders. Although there are many reasons why a person may experience such problems, having a Perfectionist approach may indeed play its part. Comments about Victoria's weight and appearance have multiplied with her ongoing weight loss. In a society where thinness is linked with beauty and success, striving to be perfect in this area may be something Victoria may have become susceptible to – particularly as she is constantly under public scrutiny. Coupled with her Perfectionist tendencies, the social pressure to appear thin may also have influenced her to lose weight. Perhaps thinness and being perfect have become inextricably linked for Victoria.

The deep-seated need to make no mistakes may also lead to a blindness to what is no longer working. For Victoria, working so hard on a music career, wanting to be the best singer and seeking approval could lead to an inability to accept her limitations. However, at the same time this reflects the key strengths of a Perfectionist: the drive to keep striving to be the very best.

THE PERFECTIONIST

NOW ABOUT YOU

Find out: are you an extreme Perfectionist thinker?

If you answer yes to more than four of these questions, you may be a Perfectionist. Here and elsewhere, answer the questions honestly in order to give yourself an accurate picture:

1. Did your parents set very high standards?
2. Are you never satisfied with your achievements?
3. Are you very good at focusing your efforts to attain a goal?
4. Do you believe that the fewer mistakes you make, the more people will like you?
5. If nine people told you that you looked beautiful or handsome, and one person said you didn't, would you spend all your time worrying about the one negative comment?
6. Do you believe that, if you fail at something, you are a failure as a person?
7. Do you set standards way beyond your reach?
8. Were you praised only when you did well?

WHY AM I AN EXTREME PERFECTIONIST THINKER?

There are many types of Perfectionist. There are those who strive for excellence because they fear failure, those who set incredibly high standards because anything less than perfection leads to feelings of dissatisfaction, and those who believe that being perfect is what is expected of them. But what lies behind these characteristics?

Family

You may have had parents who set very high standards and expected you to be nothing but the best, so that when you came second at school they felt disappointed and disapproved of your mistakes. You may also have understood from very early on in life that you had to do something pretty special to win love and attention, whether that was playing the violin or perfecting difficult ballet steps. You had to put pressure on yourself, and always aim to impress.

Faulty thinking

Psychological research on perfectionism points to faulty, rigid, all-or-nothing thinking that colours the way Perfectionists operate, and alienates or excludes others. In brief, Perfectionists have a great need to control themselves and those around them in order to avoid losing control. However, remember that even the most successful people suffer from feelings of dissatisfaction. They are constantly measuring themselves in terms of what they do but not, significantly, who they are.

THE POSITIVES AND NEGATIVES

It's worth stressing that being a Perfectionist has both its good and bad sides. It may be a wonderful experience. You may have been the one who excelled at school and

THE PERFECTIONIST

was loved by the teachers. You may be the one who is focused and motivated at work, adored by your boss. You may have a perfect body as the result of a punishing exercise schedule, and strive for excellence, always aiming to fulfil your potential. However, on the negative side, you may also feel driven by a fear that, if you stop, everything will fall apart; that people will no longer pay you any attention. You might become a workaholic and destroy close relationships, driving friends away.

Now consider this case history, used as part of Cognitive Behavioural Therapy, that describes how thoughts trigger feelings, and how feelings can lead to different kinds of behaviour.

Suzie was called in to see her boss. As soon as she heard the news, she began worrying that she'd done something wrong, and feared that she was going to be sacked. She started feeling so anxious that, instead of going in to see her boss, she didn't turn up. In short, she was engaging in all-or-nothing thinking, viewing life in extremes – things as good or bad, a success or a failure. Reality was out of focus.

What should I do if I'm like Susie?
Challenge your thinking.
  Ask what you're worried about.
  Ask how likely is it that this fear will actually happen.
  Check – is there any evidence to support your worries?
  And, by doing a reality check, you'll realise that it is your anxiety about what could go wrong that is holding you back, and not the facts themselves.

Now let's look at another case study.

Helen came from a family with very high standards. Her father was a hard worker who prided himself on always being early at work, and on never taking a day off sick in his life. Her mother was precise and ordered. So, as a child, Helen knew that being early, precise and ordered won praise. That's why, as an adult, Helen always arrived first, immaculately turned out.

But one morning her alarm didn't go off. She woke up late for work and had to rush to get ready. She arrived at work flustered and dishevelled. Helen began worrying that her colleagues now thought of her as incompetent, and felt that she had lost control. She spent the rest of the day berating herself, and being abrupt and short-tempered with colleagues. She promised herself that she would never be late again.

What should I do if I'm like Helen?

Start keeping a diary. This will help you to identify any all-or-nothing thinking, e.g. 'I've always got to be early', and enable you to notice how your thinking affects your feelings and behaviour.

Ask yourself, 'Do my colleagues really think I'm incompetent?'

Examine the emotional fall-out of being late – being upset and feeling out of control.

Check your resulting behaviour, the tendency to be abrupt and angry.

Take issue with the way you usually respond in such situations, e.g. telling yourself that 'Things will go wrong

THE PERFECTIONIST

unless I stay in control.' The problem for a Perfectionist is that this can lead to procrastination, missed deadlines and lack of motivation. The more you fear not being able to do everything perfectly well every single time, the more you will avoid completing tasks, and this can lead to anxiety and a tendency to agonise over the smallest detail. By querying your assertions, you will be able to challenge the rationale and say to yourself: where's the proof?

Every time you make an assumption about yourself, challenge it and look for the evidence to support it. Because you were late on one occasion, did it really mean that you were out of control? Be more rational; take a more balanced approach to life.

SELF-ESTEEM

Build yourself up. Surprisingly, being a Perfectionist could mean that you suffer from low self-esteem. You need to boost your confidence.

Let's imagine our case study involves someone with an exacting job and a highly critical boss, so that being late for anything means trouble. This could lead to a distorted pattern of thinking in which 'I'm early' means 'I'm good', and being late means 'I'm bad'. This would be a real confidence-knocker. And the best way to counter this effect is again to ask yourself, 'What was the worst thing that happened when I was late for work?' You will quickly realise that not only did you survive being late, but also that nothing awful happened. This will help free you from feelings of anxiety and low self-worth.

> ### CELEBRITY TIP
> Be realistic. Madonna has spent many years learning the art of yoga, and understanding what it means to her. It is clear that she hasn't done this to win any prizes or gain audience approval. She has done it for her own self-development and pleasure – and that's exactly how it should be.
>
> The trouble with being a Perfectionist is they think that, if they can't do something perfectly, then it's not worth doing at all. They set unrealistic goals. But, if you want to take up running, for example, don't start setting a goal of five miles a day, seven days a week! Plan a realistic amount, say half a mile three times a week. That way, you will end up achieving your goal and enjoying what you do.

WHO DO PERFECTIONISTS LOVE?

What types do Perfectionists go for? Let's look at three different kinds of personalities.

The powerhouse

In the past, you may have chosen a partner who was powerful, but powerful in the wrong ways. You may have been attracted to the strong, silent, macho type as you thought that what you needed most was to be kept under control. But this type is wrong for you, as they won't respond well to your vulnerability.

THE PERFECTIONIST

The pushover

You may have been attracted to more vulnerable and fragile individuals who seemed unable to function without your support. These qualities matched your desire to control everything, but the end result would be boredom. Being with someone who allowed you to be in control would also probably have left you feeling strangely lonely. So, while you carry on being invincible, you are left drained. Be realistic – avoid the needy and the helpless, because they're just reflecting what you find unacceptable in yourself.

Those you can't trust

It's often tough for Perfectionists lacking any sense of trust to let someone see that deeper, more vulnerable side, which can be destructive in a close relationship. You may tackle this problem by putting that person through multiple tests to make sure they are perfect for you. But if they can't cope with this, discard them as weak and not good enough. You see them as a failure.

If any of this applies to you, you need to look for someone who is…

> Emotionally strong and at ease when showing their emotions, but with a powerful ego.
> Not afraid to stand up to you and tell you how your behaviour manifests itself – for instance, by explaining how controlling you can be, or how your bossiness means that they occasionally feel put down.

CELEBRITY LIFE LAUNDRY

Protective towards you as you allow yourself to trust and share your life fully with someone else. At ease showing you their vulnerabilities, and who won't run a mile when you're feeling low.

2
The Serial Romantic

Being a wonderful and caring lover seems to come so naturally to you. You put the needs of your partner before your own, and create a loving, harmonious environment. But are you doing this at the expense of your own dreams and desires? Do you need to be in a relationship constantly?

To encompass the positive qualities of this kind of personality type, we have given it the name 'Serial Romantic', based on the psychological characteristics of those with a tendency towards dependency in relationships.

According to the founding father of Cognitive Therapy, Aaron T Beck, those with dependency issues in relationships tend to believe that they are helpless on their own, and seek attachment as the solution. This fear of being alone often takes root in childhood and, as Robert Bornstein writes in his book *The Dependent Personality*, this type is often a result of overprotective or authoritarian parenting. He believes that both parenting styles lead to the following results:

THE SERIAL ROMANTIC

1. A stifling of autonomous behaviour and independent thinking.
2. A tendency for children to experience difficulty in developing a sense of independence, as they are prevented from learning by trial and error.

The essential features of a dependent personality type are the excessive need to be taken care of that results in submissive and clinging behaviour. This may lead to someone forming an attachment to another person whether the relationship is good for them or not, simply as a way of avoiding the anxiety caused by being alone. So, those who have tendencies towards a dependent personality are often highly reliant on others, avoid situations that involve independent thought or conflict, and hang on to relationships, whether good or bad.

The balanced Serial Romantic is aware of their strengths – the ability to create a loving and harmonious atmosphere in relationships, as well as the ability to beware of falling into relationships in order to avoid being alone.

Bearing this in mind, let's look at three celebrities who have the dominant features of the balanced Serial Romantic.

JULIA ROBERTS – THE DARLING ROMANTIC

She is America's favourite sweetheart, Hollywood's highest-paid actress (commanding $20 million per film) and has racked up more than $1 billion in box-office sales. She has won the People's Choice award for favourite actress an impressive nine times. Her giant grin and hearty laugh are instantly recognisable, and she memorably cemented her leading-lady status by winning an Academy Award in 2001 for her performance in *Erin Brockovich*. In her emotional acceptance speech she declared, 'I love the world!'

The world's in love with Julia too, most especially a rather large group of successful and eligible men. Over the past two decades, Julia has been linked with an impressive array of male stars. Irish heartthrob Liam Neeson was Julia's first high-profile romance, in 1988. After meeting on the set of her very first film, *Satisfaction*, Julia and Liam moved in together and became engaged. Only a year later, however, Julia had moved on to her *Steel Magnolias* on-screen husband Dylan McDermott. The two became engaged in 1990, but it was over by 1991. Within months, she was dating her *Flatliners* co-star Kiefer Sutherland. Julia then dumped Kiefer just a few days before their wedding amid rumours that she had caught him in a compromising position with an exotic dancer. Kiefer seemed to confirm those rumours in a 2003 interview in which he said that he still regrets that he scuppered his chance to marry Julia. 'I loved her very, very much,' he admitted. 'There are days when I say to myself, "You were engaged to the No. 1 actress in the world and now it's over. You blew it."'

Within days of leaving Kiefer at the altar, Julia was on a plane to Dublin with one of his closest friends, actor Jason Patric. Julia and Jason had a passionate affair and moved in together in West Hollywood, but within a year they too were finished. Never one to be alone for very long, Julia embarked on another affair – this time with the actor Daniel Day Lewis. This lasted only for a few months. She was then single for just two weeks before she met the man who would be the first to get her down the aisle: Lyle Lovett.

The star couple met at a party for *The Player*, on 7 June 1993, and were married three weeks later. Lovett called their wedding 'the happiest day of my life'. The bride wore a veil and a simple white dress down to her ankles, and she was barefoot; he wore a tuxedo. At the time, Julia raved, 'He's just perfect. Just when I get used to one great thing that I've discovered [about him], I find another great thing… I feel like I'm gushing.'

Five months into the marriage, however, Lovett admitted that they had not spent more than seven days in a row together. Shortly afterwards, Julia was spotted leaving home without her wedding ring and, less than a year later, the *New York Post* published photographs of Julia dancing cheek to cheek and looking very cosy with Ethan Hawke at a trendy New York eatery. Julia's publicist insisted the two were just friends, but the photogenic twosome were spotted at a half-dozen other New York nightspots soon after. Although they were swiftly declared a hot new couple by the press, Julia denied that anything was going on. 'The facts are simple,' she said. 'I actually, for the first time in a long time, went out to dinner. Just me and some people I've worked with… The band strikes up… "Hey, you want to dance?" We all had a good time. Since when is that bad?'

CELEBRITY LIFE LAUNDRY

Denials aside, Julia and Lyle announced their separation shortly afterwards. They had been married for 21 months. After Lyle, there were rumours of several romances, none of which was serious until Julia met Benjamin Bratt in late 1997. The *Law and Order* actor and the Hollywood star were instantly smitten with each other. Julia said later that, when they met, the chemistry was so instant that 'it was like being hit with a baseball bat'. The couple were together for four years and close friends believed they would marry. Julia regularly gushed about her handsome boyfriend, telling Oprah Winfrey in 2001, 'He... just loves me unconditionally. He accepts me as a flawed individual and loves me anyway... We're just ecstatically happy... We're drunk with joy 24 hours out of the day... we're sickening.'

But while white-picket fence domesticity is many people's dream goal for a romance, it was clearly not Julia's. 'She's a bit of a gypsy,' one friend of hers said when asked about the actress's apparent reluctance to walk down the aisle with Ben. 'You can't change who you are. It's like trying to fit a square peg in a round hole.'

In spring 2001, Julia met cameraman Danny Moder on the set of *The Mexican*. At the time, he was married to a make-up artist named Vera, while Julia was still with Benjamin Bratt. In a matter of weeks, however, both Danny and Julia had broken up with their partners and were spending all their time together.

When the news broke on 28 June that Julia and Benjamin were no longer an item, she immediately denied that there was a new man in her life. While promoting

THE SERIAL ROMANTIC

America's Sweethearts, Julia willingly fielded questions about her love life, telling David Letterman that, 'I've been practising in front of the mirror: "Hi, I'm Julia. I'm single."'

Back in Los Angeles, Moder filed for divorce from his wife of four years, only six months after meeting Julia. When Julia and Ben were quietly breaking up in May 2001, 'Dan was helping her through it,' one friend of Julia's told *People* magazine. 'Vera found his cellphone bills and found out he was calling Julia every day.'

Shortly afterwards, Julia was photographed wearing a T-shirt that read 'A Low Vera', a pun some thought to be aimed at Moder's estranged wife, Vera, who was rumoured to be stalling their divorce.

Julia and Danny eventually married on 4 July 2002 in a private chapel in the grounds of Julia's New Mexico ranch. Guests included celebrity friends George Clooney and Bruce Willis. Friends of Julia told *People* magazine that this was it – he was the one. 'I think she can settle down. I think she is ready now, actually. When she finds her true love – and this looks pretty real to me – she is going to settle down and want a family.' Indeed, Julia did just that, and gave birth to twins Phinnaeus Walter and Hazel Patricia in November 2004.

And family is still the most important thing in her life. The darling of the big screen has kept a low profile since having her twins, but ventured out on stage to fulfil a long-time dream when she accepted a role in the Broadway play *Three Days of Rain*. 'It's always worth a little upheaval to make a dream come true. And I wanted this so badly. Danny was the one who encouraged me to do this show,' Julia revealed. 'I mean, I probably wouldn't have had the nerve if not for him. He kept saying, "Do it, do it, do it." I told him that our lives would change. We'd have to move to New York. And what about the kids? He said, "Let's just do it. We'll figure it out." And we did. Somehow.' She also acknowledged her husband's support in the playbill with the dedication: 'For D.M. – my courage'.

A close friend of the couple has revealed that the play brought Julia and Danny even closer together. 'I hear there have been some really excellent readings of the play at the Moder household,' the friend said. 'They seem to be the best of friends. It's so clear how happy they are together.'

So how did Julia meet current hubby Danny Moder? In a biography of Roberts – *Julia: Her Life* – writer James Spada says that Julia was hanging out with Brad Pitt on the set of the movie *The Mexican* when she saw Moder, an assistant cameraman, in the distance without his shirt. Spada, the author of biographies of Robert Redford, Ronald Reagan and Barbra Streisand, recounts that Roberts allegedly asked Pitt, 'Who's that young hunk of burning love?'

Pitt pointed out, says Spada, that Roberts was already involved with Bratt and threatened to 'tell on you'.

Undeterred, Roberts said, 'Honey, someone needs to strip that boy down and bring him to my trailer.'

Roberts didn't co-operate with Spada on the book.

THE SERIAL ROMANTIC

Julia Roberts was born on 28 October 1967 in the small town of Smyrna, Georgia. Her mother was a drama coach, and Julia grew up surrounded by actors. Her parents separated when she was three and, although she was close to her father, she didn't see him very often after the split. Tragically, he died of cancer when she was only nine. The third of four children, Julia left home as soon as she'd graduated from high school and headed for the bright lights of New York, just as her older siblings had. She knew even then that she wanted to be an actress. After a few small films, Julia landed her career-making role opposite Richard Gere in *Pretty Woman*. It made her a superstar, and she has remained one ever since.

When asked about her prolific romantic past, Julia has frequently blamed the loneliness she feels while on location. 'I happen to really like being alone,' she says. 'But I get unbelievably lonely when I go on location, sometimes for months and months at a time.' A veteran of many short-lived love affairs, Julia believes that she has learned from earlier mistakes. 'Previously, I always overcompensated in a relationship. I never realised how much of myself I was giving away until I found myself rattling around. Then you say, "Wow, I sound sort of empty." I used to get so involved in who I was with that I didn't think much of myself.'

Despite being one of the highest-paid actresses in Hollywood, Julia has publicly admitted that her personal life has been troubled by failed romance. In a rare 1998 interview with *Parade* magazine, she confessed, 'I've felt great despair in my life. What is the point of having a great job or great day or something spectacular happening if you don't have some person nearby to share it with? Unless you have someone, it's pointless. It's vapour.'

Analyse this: Julia Roberts

Julia appears to have the classic signs of a Serial Romantic. By her own admission, she seems to form emotional attachments very quickly after a close relationship ends. She herself has alluded to feeling empty when alone, and in the past has perhaps found herself overcompensating in a relationship at the expense of her own needs. At times, she appears to believe that she needs another person in her life to bring security and stability.

Julia's childhood may point to the roots of her relationship anxieties. Her parents' separation when she was three may have had a profound psychological effect on her, and her father's death when she was just nine may have reinforced this loss, perhaps creating a feeling of anxiety about getting close to someone. Julia may therefore have subconsciously decided to escape relationships before they ended, thus avoiding the potential pain of abandonment. And, in the past, by moving from one relationship to another very quickly she may have found a strategy to keep her anxiety about being alone to a minimum.

Since becoming a mother, Julia may have found a way to be a more balanced Serial Romantic, able to allow herself deeper commitment both as a mother and to a long-lasting relationship.

THE SERIAL ROMANTIC

JENNIFER LOPEZ – THE SENSUAL ROMANTIC

The showbiz world gasped in surprise when Jennifer Lopez married Marc Anthony, a virtually unknown salsa singer, in front of just 40 guests in the backyard of her Beverly Hills mansion. Despite her lavish cream Vera Wang wedding dress and the $5-million worth of jewellery she wore, what was so astonishing was that the bride had been making very public plans to marry another man only months earlier, and the proud groom had been single for a mere five days.

As an actress who commands $15 million a movie, a singer who has sold 35 million CDs and an entrepreneur with clothing and fragrance lines estimated to be worth $350 million, Jennifer has had plenty of public acclaim. She has also had a string of high-profile romances. She blames her long line of relationships on her greatest fear – being alone. 'I'm afraid of silly things, like the dark,' she confessed in one interview. 'I'm also very afraid of… How can I put this? Maybe it's because I'm from a large family, but I developed this thing where I don't want to be alone. So I'm afraid of that.' Fortunately for Jen, she hasn't had to endure much of it. Since she burst on to the Hollywood scene in 1997, Jennifer Lopez has spent virtually no time at all outside an intimate relationship.

In 1997, Jennifer married Cuban waiter and aspiring model Ojani Noa. The two met in a Miami restaurant where Ojani was working. The marriage lasted for 11 months. Following their split, Ojani went to the tabloids claiming that he ditched her after he caught her in a Los

CELEBRITY LIFE LAUNDRY

Angeles hotel room with the man who would become her next boyfriend, rap mogul Sean 'P Diddy' Combs. At the time, Jen's pals rubbished the claims saying, 'Jen has a lot of integrity and wouldn't do such a thing.'

Regardless of when it began, Jen's relationship with Combs lasted for two years, and did much to advance her career. Not only did he help to launch her music career, he also guided her in the finer points of diva-dom, including picking out that infamous green plunging-neck Versace dress she wore to the 2000 Grammy Awards. 'That dress' and the press headlines it captured around the world put Jennifer Lopez firmly on the road to superstardom. However, their romance was volatile from the outset. In an interview with *Vibe* magazine, Jen admitted that Combs cheated on her and sent her into a downward emotional dive. 'It was the first time I was with someone who wasn't faithful. After my divorce, I wasn't trying to be exclusive with anybody, but Puff came at me hard,' Lopez said. 'We started a very tumultuous affair… I was in this relationship where I was totally crying, crazy and going nuts; it put my whole life in a tailspin.'

Asked about reports of her hunting down Combs and knocking down hotel-room doors thinking he was with other women, Lopez said, 'I can't remember right now, but I won't say it didn't happen. He'd say he was going to a club for a couple of hours and never come back that night.' Jen explained that she and Combs 'broke up so many times, he didn't believe it was over when it finally ended. I had to think, do I want to be home with kids in ten years wondering where somebody is at three in the morning?'

THE SERIAL ROMANTIC

Jen has said that Combs's emotional abuse sent her straight into the arms of hubby No. 2, Cris Judd. 'Coming out of a torrid relationship, I meet this sweet person who was so refreshing,' Lopez said. 'But marriage is not just about love. We didn't have what it takes to make it work.' The two met when Cris was hired as a back-up dancer on the music video for Jen's hit single 'Love Don't Cost a Thing'. He was shy, easy-going and, by all accounts, he worshipped her. After a six-month courtship, in 2001 they married at a lavish ceremony in Donatella Versace's Como mansion. Jennifer returned from her honeymoon and went straight to work on *Gigli*. Her co-star was Hollywood hunk Ben Affleck and, unfortunately for Cris, their chemistry was intense and immediate.

Ben Affleck once described Jennifer Lopez as the 'most lethally attractive woman' he'd ever met' and, soon after filming began, the two were photographed laughing flirtatiously on set. Soon afterwards, while Jennifer was posing on the red carpet alongside hubby Cris at the opening of her Pasadena restaurant, Madre's, a stranger walked up and handed her a huge bouquet from Ben. Cris visibly fumed in front of the photographers; Jen just smiled. Weeks later, her marriage was over. It had lasted only nine months.

Jennifer's relationship with Ben Affleck led to an outrageous amount of publicity. Dubbed 'Bennifer' by the press, the couple quickly became a public phenomenon. They cavorted together in a music video for her hit 'Jenny from the Block', and she memorably dedicated a song to him on her 2002 album, *This Is Me... Then*. In 'Dear Ben', Jennifer refers to her man as 'My Lust, my Love and my King'. A much-publicised engagement soon followed, during which Jennifer described on national television every detail of Ben's proposal, as well as showing off her brand new six-carat pink diamond engagement ring. But this overexposure would cost them dearly. Their film *Gigli*, released in 2003, was savaged by critics and bombed at the box office. At the same time, cracks also began to appear in the relationship. Bennifer postponed and then cancelled their wedding, citing 'excessive media attention' as the cause.

Looking back, Jennifer says of that turbulent time, 'I wouldn't have done anything differently. I don't think I did anything wrong. I was just running around doing what I wanted – just living. And the world cared, which was sweet.'

The hit-maker began dating third husband Marc Anthony in February 2004, only a month after ending her engagement with Affleck; they were married by June. They had known each other for several years – the two did a duet on 'No Me Ames', a track from her 1999 album, *On the 6*. It was rumoured that they dated briefly at the time, and remained friends throughout their earlier marriages. Once reunited, they took only four months to tie the knot. Anthony got a quick Dominican Republic divorce from his wife, former Miss Universe Dayanara Torres, and less than a week later was married again. And their love continued to flourish amid rumours of pregnancy and adoption.

THE SERIAL ROMANTIC

A true romantic, Anthony even decided to show the world how proud and in love he was with his superstar wife by taking out a full-page ad in the American entertainment bible *Variety* to congratulate her on her Women in Film Crystal Award. In the ad, Anthony declared, 'Here's to never waking up, baby, you deserve it. I love you.'

A self-confessed romantic, Jennifer had tears in her eyes when she saw her husband's very public display of his love for her. 'He showed this to me in the car this morning and I almost started crying. It's very romantic and it's, I mean, it's so sweet I'd never expect it,' she gushed.

> **Jennifer Lopez was so stunned when an interviewer asked her how she felt about ex-fiancé Ben Affleck's baby-to-be with wife Jennifer Garner that she admitted that the subject depressed her. La Lopez, who split with her *Gigli* co-star Affleck at the beginning of last year, four months before marrying Marc Anthony – wasn't expecting that she'd have to speak about the baby news when she sat for an interview with *Elle* magazine. Blushing, Lopez said of the pregnancy, 'I hope that they're happy. You know, it's a beautiful thing. There are no hard feelings.'**
>
> **But, when *Elle* apologised for raising the subject, Lopez, who later admitted that becoming a mother is one of her ultimate dreams, responded, 'Yeah, you depressed me.'**
>
> *Boston Herald*, **30 July 2005**

CELEBRITY LIFE LAUNDRY

Jennifer needs romance in her life – and lucky for her, she seems to have finally found a partner who needs it too. When asked what it was like being married to the superstar, Marc Anthony summed it up well: 'What I would say is just that it sort of feels like I'm living in a fairy tale.'

Jennifer Lynn Lopez was born on 24 July 1969 to Puerto Rican parents in the Bronx area of New York. Her father, David, was a computer technician, and her mother, Guadalupe, taught at kindergarten. The middle of three sisters, Jennifer took singing and dancing lessons from the age of five. Even as a young woman, she had one priority – making it in show business. 'You sacrifice relationships. You sacrifice seeing your family as much as you'd like to. You sacrifice weekends. You sacrifice having the normal pleasures that everyone else takes for granted. You give that up, and it doesn't matter to you when you're in your twenties. You just go, "OK. I don't care. I'm doing my thing." Then all of a sudden, you're like, "I missed out on a lot."'

The superstar has said her marriage to Marc Anthony marks 'phase two' of her life, and that through this marriage she is reinventing her turbulent love life and wiping away her romantic past. 'I feel like it's a new beginning. Like everything I did before really doesn't matter. Maybe I was a little bit careless in the past. I'm not a perfect person. I make mistakes. I just feel like I'm in a better place about who I am. I follow my heart. That's the one thing I can say about myself. And I love that about myself.'

THE SERIAL ROMANTIC

Analyse this: Jennifer Lopez

Jennifer seems to embody the key characteristics of a Serial Romantic. She admits to a fear of being alone, seems to move seamlessly from one relationship to another, turns to her lovers for support, advice and security, and even admits to being driven into the arms of a new lover for comfort when an old one has let her down. It is almost as if she feels that this is her only choice.

At times she puts herself in a submissive position, as she did with P Diddy. One has the sense that she elevates her lovers above herself, and by putting them on a pedestal she imbues them with more power. Is this her way of fending off being alone?

Her eagerness to announce her intentions to marry so soon after meeting someone new has resulted in a repeating pattern. Perhaps this has been an attempt to maintain and preserve the relationship, even though some of her choices may not have been good for her, and have certainly surprised those who know her. Has this been a result of an emotional need to stave off anxiety about being left alone?

BRAD PITT – THE DEVOTED ROMANTIC

When Brad Pitt married Jennifer Aniston on 29 July 2000 in a million-dollar ceremony in Malibu, they certainly did it in style. The happy couple were surrounded by some 200 guests, 50,000 flowers, four bands, a gospel choir and fireworks. After the honeymoon, the lovebirds were spotted all over Hollywood holding hands and kissing.

CELEBRITY LIFE LAUNDRY

When Jen showed up on the set of British hit movie *Snatch*, in which Brad starred, in 2000, one crew member told the press, 'As soon as they saw each other their faces lit up. They kissed each other really tenderly. It was obvious they were madly in love.'

During this time, Brad said of Jen in a *Rolling Stone* interview, 'She's complicated, she's wise, she's fair and she has great empathy for others... and she's just so cool.'

In 2001, after five weeks of filming *The Mexican* in remote Real de Catorce, producer Lawrence Bender said of Brad, 'He was like, "I gotta get back and see my girl." They're just lovebirds.'

At the time, Brad revealed in one interview, 'I'm pretty much mush. I like love. I'm a huge believer in love and why two people come together and what the potentialities are of that. So I call myself sappy, but I'm not... I think there's huge value in love.' He added, 'The only thing that life has taught me up to this point is that anything can happen. And everything can change at any given moment.' And unfortunately for Brad and Jen, it did.

The pair announced their separation on 7 January 2005. Rumours had been circulating for months that there was trouble in paradise, but now it was official: Hollywood's golden couple were no more. In a subsequent interview, Brad explained, 'The idea that marriage has to be for all time – that I don't understand. It's talked about like it failed, I guess because it wasn't flawless,' he mused. 'Me, I embrace the messiness of life. I find it so beautiful, actually.' As for their split, 'We've done it our way, and I love her for that. We've kept the love we have for each other.'

Rumours were soon circulating of an off-screen chemistry between the still-married Brad and his *Mr and Mrs Smith* co-star Angelina Jolie, and before long photographs of the new couple relaxing on a beach in Kenya were published around the world. Angelina denied that anything had happened while Brad was still married, stating, 'To be intimate with a married man, when my own father cheated on my mother, is not something I could forgive.'

Brad complained that Angelina was simply misunderstood. 'I've never seen someone so misperceived in the press,' he said. 'Jolie's really a delightful human being, a dedicated mother and really quite normal. [She's] dedicated to her work with the UN. There's actually a real lightness to her.'

Regardless of when their affair began, it is clear that once again Brad Pitt was in love. And it was Angelina who would go on to fulfil his lifelong dream. Shortly before announcing his separation from Jennifer Aniston, Pitt, close to tears, revealed in an interview that he longed for a family. 'I'm going to say it – kids, family, I am thinking family,' he revealed. 'Yes, I have got family on the mind. Jen and I have been working something out. Little girls, they just crush me – they break my heart.'

Unfortunately for Jennifer, she would not be the one to give Brad that little girl he so desperately desired. Angelina gave him an instant family with son Maddox and daughter Zahara and also made his dream come true by giving birth

CELEBRITY LIFE LAUNDRY

to his biological daughter Shiloh Nouvel Jolie-Pitt on 25 May 2006 in Namibia. So desperate was the world to see the offspring of this outrageously sexy pair that Shiloh's first pictures sold for over $7.5 million, a sum that Brad and Angelina promptly donated to charity.

Brad Pitt has been named *People* magazine's 'Sexiest Man Alive' not once but twice in the space of his 20-year career, and, at 41, he still gets women going. His appeal goes deeper than his piercing blue eyes, or strong, handsome physique. He is a ladies man, but he's no Casanova. Brad is more your dedicated Romeo, a one-woman man with a strong romantic side. When Brad Pitt falls in love, he falls deeply.

A long line of women have succumbed to Brad's charms. Most were co-stars – it seems Brad has a habit of taking his love scenes home with him. His first Hollywood romance was in 1988 with his *Dallas* co-star Shalane McCall. The two were paired as a couple on the hit Texas oil drama, and were quickly dating off screen as well. She was 16; he was 24. Shortly afterwards, in 1989, Brad began seeing Robin Givens (the future Mrs Mike Tyson) after meeting her during a guest spot on her sitcom *Head of the Class*. Their affair came to an abrupt end a few weeks later when boxer Mike – then married to Givens – started hammering on the front door demanding to be let in. 'I had to run out of the back door pulling my pants up while Robin stalled Mike at the front. He would've killed me,' recalled Brad.

'It's hard to look at Brad without imagining him in bed,' Givens commented wryly.

THE SERIAL ROMANTIC

While starring in the 1989 comedy-thriller *Cutting Class*, Brad fell for his co-star Jill Schoelen. The relationship lasted for nine months, until she dumped him. According to Brad, Jill broke his heart after he had jetted off to visit her on location in Hungary only to discover she'd dropped him for the movie's director. 'It was one of my worst moments,' he confessed. 'You don't forget something like that and maybe I've never quite got over the feeling of humiliation. I have to put it down to experience, but that's very hard. It may have affected the way I've conducted some relationships since.'

Brad quickly bounced back while making the 1990 TV movie *Too Young to Die* with his co-star Juliette Lewis. They were together for three years, memorably co-starring in the 1993 film *Kalifornia* as a gun-toting serial killer and his white-trash girlfriend. Their split in 1994 was heartbreaking for both, with Juliette commenting, 'The thing is, Brad does not know how heartbreakingly beautiful he is.'

After Juliette, Brad got back together with an ex-girlfriend called Jitka Pohlodek. She was an 18-year-old aspiring actress from Little Rock Arkansas who Brad picked up while she was working at an Alamo rental car counter at Los Angeles International airport. She told one paper, 'He tracked me down and called me at home to ask me out.' Within months of splitting with Juliette, Brad and Jitka were back on and living together. Although the romance ended for good in 1994, Jitka still considers Pitt a 'good, good friend. I don't know if people realise what a down-to-earth person Brad is. Does he pick up the cheque on dates? Of course. Open doors for women? Of course. But he is also a very sexy man, very romantic. I'm not going to go there except to say that he was. Very.'

In 1995, Brad began filming *Se7en* and fell madly in love with his willowy co-star Gwyneth Paltrow. The blonde pair quickly became the most glamorous couple Hollywood had seen in decades. Brad bought Gwyneth a $25,000 engagement ring and took several months off to join her in London, where she was working. When he accepted the Golden Globe Award for Best Supporting Actor for *12 Monkeys*, he praised Gwyneth, calling her 'my angel, the love of my life'.

Their affair was passionate – the lovebirds were memorably photographed romping in the nude while on holiday in the Caribbean. But six months after their engagement, the wedding was off. No public explanation was given. Whatever really happened, Gwyneth seems willing to take the blame, for when she referred to their break-up she said, 'I was the architect of my own misery. I just made a big mess out of it. My heart sort of broke that day and it will never be the same. I think you have to keep yourself intact in order to have a healthy relationship, and I didn't.'

For his part, Brad maintained a gentlemanly silence for months afterwards, finally offering a non-committal 'You figure it out' to *Vanity Fair* magazine.

Still nursing a broken heart, Brad played the field. He was linked with a string of beautiful women including little-known actress Katja Garnier. At the time he

THE SERIAL ROMANTIC

Brad Pitt loves Valentine's Day. In 2001, he filled then wife Jennifer Aniston's dressing room on the set of *Friends* with 1,500 roses and used petals to display the message: 'I love my wife.'

Back when Brad was dating Gwyneth Paltrow, he was already a romantic. For Gwynnie's 24th birthday, Brad arranged a surprise party at the hotel Valle Andino in Uspallata, a small town in the Andes three miles from the set of his film *Seven Years in Tibet*. 'He started blowing up balloons with some friends, and we all helped him,' said one guest. 'He decorated the whole room with flowers – roses, orchids – they were everywhere. And he made a sign with sparkling letters that read, "Happy Birthday, Gwyneth." She is a lucky woman, and he a lucky man.'

'They are like adolescents in love,' says Dr Horacio Cervo Zenie, Pitt's physician on the set. Zenie has seen them 'feeding each other, kissing, doing things that people who are madly in love do. As soon as Gwyneth would arrive on the set, Brad would rush off and give her a big hug. You can't help but admire that.'

Adds Maria Teresa de Barbeira, a Mendoza restaurant owner who cooked dozens of Italian-style meals (including one of his favourites, paglia e fieno) for Pitt, 'It is like they are acting out a romantic scene in a movie. But it is real life and they are not acting. They are just very much in love.'

revealed, 'That sex-symbol thing makes me vomit. How does anyone expect me to have a relationship with a girl these days?' Shortly after this rant, the two split up.

Brad Pitt grew up far from the glittering lights of Hollywood. The oldest of three children, he was born on 18 December 1963 in Shawnee, Oklahoma. His mother, Jane, was a teacher and his dad, Bill, worked for a trucking company. He was a popular boy, good at tennis and won the 'Best Dressed' vote in high school. He studied advertising and journalism at Missouri University but, just two weeks before graduating, he took off, abandoning his degree, and headed for Los Angeles.

Intent on becoming a star, he quickly signed up for acting lessons. Unsurprisingly, his female classmates were eager to work with the handsome 20-year-old. A bit part in *Dallas* led to his breakthrough role in the box-office hit *Thelma & Louise*. Although he was on screen for only 14 minutes, Brad's portrayal of a sexy cowboy thief made him an overnight star.

Superstardom doesn't seem to have toughened up the sensitive man who once described himself as 'hard as a box of Kleenex tissues'. An incurable romantic, Brad has adopted something of a melancholy view towards life. 'I'm sure there are some rude awakenings yet to come. But I like it like that. I like the unknown. It's just more vibrant that way,' he once revealed, adding, 'I'm not a big proponent of happiness. I think it's highly overrated. I think misery is underrated.'

THE SERIAL ROMANTIC

And as for his views on love, serial monogamist Brad believes it is all important. 'Love? Love is everything,' he says. 'I have a friend who works with the terminally ill and he says that people on their deathbeds don't talk about what car they drove or what they did, only about their loves or regrets for the loves that they let go by or didn't take a chance on. That says a lot to me about what matters at the end of the day – the connections we make with other souls.'

Analyse this: Brad Pitt

Brad has no problem attracting women, and seems to move from one co-star to the next, although he seems to have found happiness with Angelina Jolie at present. One of the features of a Serial Romantic is a need to be attached to another person in order to avoid being alone. This dependency may have found Brad at the mercy of his love interest at times, resulting in his being unceremoniously dumped. His response seems to have been to move swiftly into the arms of another.

Interestingly, Brad's ex-lovers, on the whole, seem to remember him fondly, perhaps another telltale sign of a Serial Romantic. This type can make great lovers, as they aim to minimise conflict, maximise harmony and work hard to preserve the relationship. However, Serial Romantics experience great anxiety because, when they are single, they possess deep fears about being alone, and when with a partner they are terrified of being rejected. It is a vicious circle.

Brad, in love, is dedicated and committed. He may

worry about losing his lover, or being single, though. Maybe for him the biggest challenge is to be happy in his own company.

NOW ABOUT YOU

Find out: are you an extreme Serial Romantic?

If you answer yes to four or more of these questions, you may be an extreme Serial Romantic:

1. Do you often feel more confident when you are in a relationship?
2. Do you feel desperate to get into another relationship quickly when a close relationship ends?
3. Does spending time alone make you feel anxious?
4. Do you believe that you're helpless if left alone?
5. Do you sometimes feel that you'll do anything to keep your lover?
6. Was your mother or father very protective of you?
7. Do you sometimes feel anxious for no reason, and worry that your partner will abandon you?
8. Did you grow up in a strict family environment?

If your score indicates you might well fall into this category, it's time to ask yourself: 'Why am I an extreme Serial Romantic?' The two main factors are:

THE SERIAL ROMANTIC

Family
According to research, people who grow up to depend on significant relationships come from homes where they either felt overprotected, or where the parental stance was very authoritarian. And a lack of structured learning when young, e.g. by trial and error, not only discourages autonomous thinking but encourages dependency tendencies. Such strong influences can make you believe you need the support and guidance of another person in order to cope with the world. As a result, you may have constantly searched for people who made you feel cared for.

Faulty thinking
As an adult, you may find that you need company to avoid being by yourself, believing that you can't cope alone, even though you may recognise that your partner isn't ultimately the right person for you. This belief may lead to serial relationship behaviour, as you continue to see yourself as inadequate without a partner.

The positives and negatives
Being a Serial Romantic can seem thrilling when you have the constant euphoria of meeting and falling in love with somebody new. For you, falling in love often happens very quickly and you soon believe that your new partner can offer you everything that you believe you need. But there is a negative side.

Problems begin when this relationship goes through change and conflict, or your partner is unable to meet your needs, and you start to feel anxious, troubled and insecure. If the relationship then ends, instead of spending time alone to reflect on what might have happened, you quickly search out the next person who can fulfil your emotional needs. This gives immediate, short-term comfort but, in the long term, means that you may get stuck repeating the same psychological pattern.

Let's look at a case history: Maddy's relationship ended recently and she feels terrible, missing the closeness and bond she had with her ex. Her friends invite her to a dinner party to cheer her up, and she meets Dave. He pays her compliments all evening, makes her laugh and makes her feel good about herself again.

Maddy starts thinking, 'Dave makes me feel so great. He's perfect. I really think he's the one who can take care of me.' She quickly jumps into a new relationship with him, and makes plans to move in with him just a few weeks after their first meeting.

What should I do if I'm like Maddy?
Ask yourself:
How well do I really know this guy?
Would it hurt me to wait a while before we move in together?
Would it be wise to move in with a stranger?
Am I only half a person when I'm single?
By slowing yourself down, you will start to think through the consequences of your actions. Are you repeating a pattern of 'out of the frying pan and into the fire'?

THE SERIAL ROMANTIC

Now read Jo's story, which adds a further twist. Jo comes from a large, close family, with lots of brothers and sisters. Her parents were loving, but overprotective. She was never allowed to go on school trips in case something happened. And when Jo was a teenager, her dad wouldn't let her go out with boys, and was very strict about her continuing ballet classes long after she got bored with them. When she wanted to leave home and get a job, her father encouraged her to go to university and study law, which she did.

When Jo finally left home, she found it difficult to make simple decisions, often ringing her parents to ask their opinion. She hated being single, and often dated men just so that she didn't have to be alone. When she was in a relationship, Jo felt safe and secure, and didn't mind her boyfriend making most of the decisions – where to go for dinner, and which film to watch, for example. At 29, however, Jo found herself single again and feeling anxious, but not really knowing why.

What should I do if I'm like Jo?
Here are four steps you could take:

1. Examine your long-held beliefs about love and relationships. A great way to start your detective work is to keep a diary. Write down the history of your relationships, starting with the first person you ever went out with. What were your hopes for the relationship? What went wrong? How did you deal with it? Then take a step back. What messages did you receive from your

parents? By tackling these questions, you will start to notice the ideas that shape your attitudes to love, and you'll be more conscious of how you decide who to date.

2. Develop self-sufficiency. One of the hardest things for you is spending periods of time on your own; you'd rather be with somebody to avoid feelings of abandonment or separation-anxiety. But in order to break the cycle of high-dependency relationships, it's crucial that you take time out and learn to be by yourself.

You may believe that without somebody in your life you are going to be depressed, feeling lonely and insecure. If so, challenge that assumption. Time spent alone is invaluable. It gives you a chance to examine who you are, and an opportunity to feel complete when you're by yourself. Start small. At the weekend, plan a day-trip somewhere on your own. Appreciate how enjoyable it can be.

3. Stop and think. Breaking the cycle of serial relationships requires you to stand back and think about what it is you are doing. If you break up with somebody and then feel the immediate need to be close with someone else, you may be caught up in an addictive pattern. Ask yourself, 'What is it that I can't do without from this person? And do I believe that without them I'm inadequate?'

This will help open your eyes to what you think may be missing in you. Note that healthy love means that both of you are equal in the relationship, but unhealthy love means being needy of your partner, either

THE SERIAL ROMANTIC

expecting them to meet your needs or being happy meeting theirs so that you don't lose them. Either way, the relationship is doomed; it relies on both of you staying locked in this pattern.

4. Stop being idealistic. Placing high expectations on your partner to fulfil your needs is fatal. You may have a tendency to see them as being perfect because they appear to offer you everything you need. And you may find that at times you are the one prepared to do anything to give them what they want so that you don't have to be alone. This might mean that you are taken for granted.

The solution is to give yourself a reality check. Challenge your thinking. Seeing people more clearly for who they are will help you formulate more genuine and grounded relationships.

CELEBRITY TIP

Brad took the positive step of undergoing therapy to understand his patterns. You could do the same. Ask for help and examine your repeated patterns, and learn to break the chain with the help of a qualified therapist.

THE SERIAL ROMANTIC IN LOVE

Let's look at three kinds of influences on the kind of attachments Serial Romantics form:

The fantasy

In the past, your relationships may have started off as wonderful, even perfect. You had an idealised and romanticised view of your partner, who appeared to be everything you ever wanted. You felt whole and complete when together, believing the relationship had real security.

The honeymoon

Perhaps you worked very hard to recreate the 'honeymoon' period, trying to return to a time when your partner was everything you needed and you were at your happiest.

Needy love

Do you think you made chaotic choices, even getting close to someone who you knew was wrong for you, preferring that to the thought of being alone?

If any of this sounds familiar, here's your biggest challenge. Start believing that you are in control of your own future. First, that means building your self-confidence. Being someone who can cope, rather than someone who is incapable, is crucial to your gaining emotional strength.

THE HEALTHY RELATIONSHIP

Having done all this, it's time to embark on a relationship through a position of equality and not anxiety. A lover in such a healthy relationship would encourage you to

THE SERIAL ROMANTIC

embrace your independence, and discourage any dependency behaviour. In particular, your lover/partner...

1. *Won't abuse your trust, but will encourage you to take steps to increase your confidence in the relationship.*
2. *Won't be afraid or threatened by you when you assert yourself and sometimes stand back, pointing out their negative behaviour.*
3. *Will invite you to take more responsibility for your decisions without being critical or overprotective.*

This healthy new relationship will enable you to find your confidence and minimise your fears.

3
The Thrill Seeker

They are fun to be around, and their energy is infectious, yet they can be impulsive at times, taking risks that could place them in danger. According to research by the eminent psychologist Marvin Zuckerman, common characteristics of Thrill Seekers include...

1. Showing a willingness to take physical risks and participate in high-risk sports.
2. A desire for experiences that reflect the need for what's new and exciting.
3. 'Disinhibition', which Zuckerman links to a willingness to take social and health risks, including binge drinking and/or unprotected sex.
4. Boredom susceptibility, which is connected to an intolerance of monotony.

In his article 'Thrill seekers thrive on the scary', Richard Trubo draws attention to a comment by Frank Farley, who has made a series of studies of devoted roller-coaster riders: 'There's almost nothing else, including sex, that can

THE THRILL SEEKER

match it in terms of incredible sensory experience that the body is put through.' He adds, 'Sky divers will tell you it's the thrill and the rush, and a little element of fear, that motivates them to push themselves to the extreme.'

But while sensation seeking may produce wonderful pioneers, emergency workers or policemen, research also indicates that, in its extreme form, other Thrill Seekers may fall prey to alcohol or drug problems, or may even become sex addicts or criminals.

Balanced Thrill Seekers are tuned into their many strengths and do not deny themselves their adventurous spirit, yet also have a strong awareness of the consequences of risk-taking behaviour. This puts them in the position of being able to confidently try new things, while having the ability to err on the side of caution.

With this in mind, let's look at three celebrities who best reflect the dominant features of a balanced Thrill Seeker.

ANGELINA JOLIE – THE OUTSPOKEN THRILL SEEKER

In Hollywood, when celebrity mums-to-be approach their due date, they quietly check into LA's Cedars-Sinai Medical Center, reserving the finest birthing suites in the world, decorated in soft, plush furnishings to rival the top five-star hotel suites with enough space to hold a nervous dad and family members as well as the requisite entourage of publicists, assistants and managers. These mums, who are 'too posh to push', schedule a C-section followed by a discreet tummy tuck by a top surgeon and bring in hair colourists, make-up artists and trainers to prepare them for their first post-baby photo deal.

Angelina Jolie was never going to go for that. This mother of three hasn't merely given birth, she has literally rescued her children from desperate conditions in Third World countries. For her first biological child with boyfriend Brad Pitt, Angie skipped the fancy hospital suite and instead flew to the small nation of Namibia where, surrounded by her nearest and dearest, she prepared to give birth at a seaside resort. After some complications, Angie ended up having a Caesarean in a small but well-respected private hospital in Swakopmund, Namibia. 'I was sure everything was going to go right and, at the last minute, I became the mom who was sure everything was going to go wrong,' Angelina admitted later. 'You know, because you're there for the birth, which I wasn't for my first two kids, you're just suddenly terrified that they're not gonna take a first breath. That was my whole focus. I just wanted to hear her cry.'

It should have come as no surprise that Angelina gave birth for the first time in such dramatic circumstances. After all, this is the same woman who memorably burst on to movie screens as the voluptuous adventurer Lara Croft in *Tomb Raider*, quickly cementing her place as every adolescent boy's fantasy. Here was a woman who rode horses, motorcycles and jet skis with sexy aplomb while wielding knives and guns like a real commando – all the while smiling seductively with her full lips. She was every inch the superhero.

Angelina's real-life antics, including dabbling in

THE THRILL SEEKER

lesbianism and admitting to a fascination with blood, branded her a true rebel who stood out from the hordes of carefully crafted stars so typical of Hollywood. For many years, she refused to hire a publicist and seemed to thrive on her frankness with her fans and the media.

Angelina has been very open about her difficult childhood. Her father, the actor Jon Voight, left her mother, the French actress Marcheline Bertrand, when Angelina was a baby. The actress has admitted that she has since found it difficult to be touched, saying, 'It was part of not wanting to be caged in.' There were years of drug use and self-mutilation. 'I had a lot inside me. Like a lot of people, I didn't have any outlets or anything. I collected knives... for some reason, the ritual of having cut myself and feeling pain maybe, feeling alive, feeling some kind of release... I loved being free.'

In the wake of her parents' divorce, Angelina became very close to her brother, James. She shocked the world in 2000 when she brought him on stage to accept her award at the Golden Globes and provocatively locked lips with him. She later answered inevitable speculation on the subject of incest with typical candour: 'If I were doing that, I'd say it. Everyone knows that about me.'

In fact, Angelina has always been incredibly candid about her riotous sex life. She had her first live-in boyfriend at 14, and has been open about her affairs with women as well as men. When asked how she learned the facts of life, she once said, 'I kind of fell right into them.' She was only 20 when she wed *Trainspotting* star Jonny Lee Miller. At the ceremony, Angelina gave new meaning

CELEBRITY LIFE LAUNDRY

According to Angelina Jolie's former lesbian lover Jenny Shumuzu, their sex life was volatile: 'It's not so much we were dressed in leather capes and masks and there were chains. It was emotional. I would restrain her with my arms but we didn't get into buying stuff. We just used whatever props were available if we wanted to. She was a collector of knives and taught me about them.' As for the chances of Angelina embracing monogamy, Jenny is sceptical: 'Maybe she would settle down and be with one person but I think she goes looking for excitement all the time. Her passion is people and it's hard to just settle down with one person when you have a whole world in front of you. I'm not saying she sleeps with a lot of people. But I can't imagine her just being married and being happy.

'She's always had lovers that she relies on. If she can ring you and you can meet up, then she can take care of her sexual needs,' said the model. 'Whenever she calls me up, I visit her. It's not always the case that we have sex. Sometimes we go to her property in Cambodia and explore the jungle.' As for the chances of Angelina and Brad Pitt working out – Jenny (who has known Angie for 11 years) doesn't think it'll last. 'I don't think there is any way of controlling Angelina. She's not going to be a housewife.'

to the term 'modern bride' when she rejected a traditional wedding dress for rubber pants and a white shirt that had Miller's name scrawled in blood across the back.

The couple soon split and Angelina moved on to her *Pushing Tin* co-star Billy Bob Thornton. At the time they met, Billy Bob was living with long-term girlfriend Laura Dern, but he eventually left Laura for Angelina. Inevitably, a media frenzy erupted. Dern herself had thought she and Thornton were still an item, and later commented, 'I left my home to work on a movie, and while I was away my boyfriend got married and I never heard from him again.'

Angelina's wedding to Billy Bob (her second, his fifth) was far removed from the obligatory glitz and glamour you might expect from a pair of A-listers. The couple headed to Las Vegas for a quickie. Angelina wore blue jeans and Billy Bob splashed out on a $29 ring, from a jeweller selling rings on the street. 'It's amazing that we actually leave the bedroom – ever,' Angelina once said. 'I think I'm going to die every few minutes [when we're having sex].'

The newlyweds moved into a $4-million estate in Beverly Hills, which had multiple bedrooms, a swimming pool and a weapons room stocked with knives and guns. They also installed an indoor Velcro wall so that they could run at it at full speed and stick to it. Much was written about the pendants the lovers wore, which were filled with each other's blood. Angelina's explanation for them was simple: 'If I could drink his blood, if I could devour every part of him, I would. He's my soul.' And there was more to come.

CELEBRITY LIFE LAUNDRY

Angelina had the words 'Quod me nutrit me destruit' ('What feeds me destroys me') tattooed on her stomach, and 'Billy Bob' etched in a place so private it could be neither seen nor removed. Her marital bed had 'Till the end' daubed above it in blood, and her anniversary gift to Billy was matching cemetery plots. Yet, despite all this shared eccentricity, the marriage ultimately failed.

Angelina's subsequent romance with Hollywood heartthrob Brad Pitt sent shock waves around the world. When rumours started to surface about the two stars during filming of *Mr and Mrs Smith*, Brad and wife Jennifer Aniston were still Hollywood's Golden Couple. And while both Brad and Angelina deny that a sexual relationship took place before his marriage was over, they have not left each other's side since. Angelina, who has her pilot's licence, encouraged Brad to fly, and the actor has been dutifully taking lessons. The pair has since settled down into a domestic routine with their adopted children. According to sources on the 2005 set of Brad's film *Jesse James*, Angelina joined him nearly every day for lunch and was constantly blowing him kisses off-camera.

Angelina's freedom of expression has paid off professionally. The star won an Academy Award at just 24 for her performance in *Girl, Interrupted*, in which she played a self-destructive mental patient whose psychological fractures draw parallels with the actress's own life. And she is as fearless with her body as she is with her emotions. Her success as Lara Croft in *Tomb Raider* was not just down to her intoxicating sensuality and piercing stares. She trained rigorously for three months

THE THRILL SEEKER

before the film, working on martial arts, bungee jumping and even husky-dog racing, and brought the action character to life by doing her own stunts and fight scenes.

Stunt co-ordinators are known to be fearful of working with this adrenaline junkie. When she was 20, and on the set of *Foxfire*, Angelina famously unhooked her safety harness while dangling from a bridge. 'It was hindering me,' Angelina explained afterwards. 'The story about that harness got to every stunt person I've ever worked with. So now, every movie, they keep double-checking my safeties all the time.'

Gradually, though, there seemed to be a shift in her personal priorities. After spending months in Cambodia for *Tomb Raider*, Angelina was moved to adopt a child and took home her new son, Maddox, from a local orphanage. She seemed to be changing from her raucous, dangerous ways into a mother who took her job seriously. Maddox and Angelina became inseparable. She has said, 'I'm a mother now, which is a lot wilder and more dangerous than anything I was doing as a teenager. My life has actually gotten more wild. It's just not as chaotic and disorganised any more. It's more adult, with responsibilities.' And the actress is characteristically keen to take motherhood to the extreme. She has already adopted another orphan, from Africa, and plans to adopt many more from countries all over the world. She was recently overheard saying that she and Brad want 13 children in total.

Angelina seems to have channelled her desire to push boundaries from a personal focus into a global direction. She has followed her heart and thirst for adventure by visiting refugee camps and war-torn areas as a goodwill ambassador for the United Nations. She gives a percentage of her income to Third World Aid, committed $5 million of her own money to establish a Cambodian wildlife preserve and another $10,000 to rebuild a hospital in Sri Lanka, and has also been spotted lobbying in Washington to help immigrant orphans in the USA. As she herself has said, 'Nowadays I have a home in the jungle in Cambodia and we have just cleared 48 landmines from my property. That, to me, takes guts. Or going to the borders of certain countries, which aren't the safest, because I care about it. The real aid workers who risk their lives every day – they know wild. They know bold.'

Analyse this: Angelina Jolie

Angelina appears to possess key ingredients of the classic Thrill Seeker, being both daring and fearless. She seems to thrive on, and come alive by, putting herself in heart-stopping situations. But while she may have been born with thrill-seeking tendencies, her environment would also have influenced this side of her personality. And her early childhood difficulties could have had an effect, helping shape her responses to difficult feelings. Later, in adulthood, she may have used her fearless risk-taking, acting and her outrageous relationships to communicate and handle her frustrations and rage.

Angelina's openness about her self-harming was high risk, brave and revealing. By being so honest and open about her behaviour, she may have given herself the

THE THRILL SEEKER

psychological liberation to express something that is often a hidden, secretive habit. By being so open about an often hidden problem, she may have used her ability to take risks for a greater good.

Thrill Seekers often seek each other out for relationships; they see in the other the thrill and excitement of life. However, this can lead to destructive relationships as neither party is able to rein in the other, and instead they may actually push each other's boundaries too far back. This is graphically illustrated in Angelina's history of colourful relationships (although it will be interesting to see what happens with Serial Romantic Brad).

By channelling her energies into action films, Angelina is using her sensation-seeking side positively, to express herself in a relatively safe, controlled fashion. Raising children and involving herself in charitable work, albeit charities that take her to dangerous places, may represent a new mature Angelina who, in the very act of putting the needs of others first, is behaving in a less impulsive and less reckless way.

KATE MOSS – THE CONSUMMATE THRILL SEEKER

Those grainy images of Kate Moss allegedly snorting cocaine spread around the world in an instant. There sat the world's most famous fashion icon, whose face has graced magazine covers and billboards from New York to Tokyo, slouched over in a dingy, dimly lit recording studio, apparently cutting up lines of coke. Within days, fashion firms H&M, Burberry and Chanel announced they would no longer be requiring her services. Kate was quickly vilified in the world's press as a selfish party animal and an unfit mother to her three-year old daughter Lila Grace. Acquaintances came out of the woodwork in order to share their best stories about the star and the British tabloids swiftly dubbed her 'Cocaine Kate'. Meanwhile, Kate quietly checked herself into the Meadows, a tough rehab centre in Arizona known for helping celebrities with addiction. How the mighty had fallen. For those who knew Kate, however, this was all far from shocking.

Discovered at JFK airport at the age of 14, Kate went from schoolgirl to fronting billboards for Calvin Klein within the space of a few short years. At only five-foot six, and wafer thin, she inspired a virtual revolution in the modelling industry. Kate was frequently seen staring back from the covers of fashion bible *Vogue*, as well as *Harper's Bazaar* and *Elle*. She epitomised the look of the moment: a grungy-looking waif, with a fresh-faced pout. The era of the Amazonian supermodel was officially over. Shuttled to parties and premieres while still in her teens, Kate loved the lifestyle, and she grew up fast. But, just as Kate was struggling to adjust to her newfound fame, her family fell apart. Her parents' divorce literally split her world in half. She remained with her mother Linda and her new partner, while her younger brother Nick chose to live with their father, Peter.

Aged 20, Kate began a tempestuous four-year relationship with bad-boy screen idol Johnny Depp. But Depp's alleged drug use and violent temper did little to help her cope with her stressful lifestyle. Depp was said to

THE THRILL SEEKER

have broken Kate's heart when he dumped her in 1998 for the French singer Vanessa Paradis, and friends claim that she has never really trusted a man since.

Shortly after her break-up with Johnny, at 25, Kate reached out for help. The model paid her first visit to The Priory clinic, claiming she was 'partied out' and suffering from 'exhaustion'. It was later revealed that she had received treatment there for alcohol and drug abuse. According to reports, Kate admitted that, for a long time, her use of drugs and champagne helped her to balance her busy schedule with the pace and partying of the A-list fashion world.

Many observers wrongly assumed that Kate would slow down with the birth of daughter Lila Grace. It was not to be. The model caused an outcry when she was photographed smoking while four months pregnant, and was rumoured to have rejected pleas by Lila's father Jefferson Hack to marry him and have more children. In fact, the celebration of Lila's christening became a two-day champagne-fuelled bash featuring a collection of famed party animals, including Marianne Faithfull, Jude Law's estranged wife Sadie Frost, and rock star Noel Gallagher's ex Meg Mathews. The setting was Walnut Tree Cottage, a 300-year-old home that Kate was renting in Gloucestershire. When retired merchant banker Sir Rowland Whitehead was eventually handed his house back, he found damaged light-fittings, soiled armchairs, a dented stove and a radiator that was falling off the bathroom wall. 'It is not the house that we had two years ago,' he told the papers.

CELEBRITY LIFE LAUNDRY

Kate's 30th birthday party had the theme 'Beautiful and Damned', and captured headlines around the world. It was a theme that seemed seedily appropriate for Kate and her close-knit circle of friends. Despite tight security and attempts to ensure her privacy, stories trickled out from various sources at the party who claimed they'd observed wild sexual orgies and drug-taking.

While Kate has amassed a personal fortune estimated at £50 million, the fashion plate is rarely seen lunching at trendy restaurants or gliding across red carpets. In the recent past, Kate was far more likely to be spotted at one of London's less reputable nightclubs, hanging on the arm of a skinny, pale-skinned, unkempt singer called Pete. Her recent fling with Pete Doherty, the former Libertines star,

> **In May 2006, Kate Moss was photographed attacking a photographer hours after her former lover, heroin addict Pete Doherty, was pictured leaving her house. The supermodel lashed out when the cameraman tried to snap her leaving a friend's home in north London. According to an eyewitness, 'She came out and went straight for him. She knocked the camera out of his hand and started stamping on the lens cover. She started to kick and punch him. She came out and gave a girly fit at him. She completely lost it.' The photographer complained of a sore leg but is not believed to be pressing charges. Kate's outburst was mildly successful: she broke his lens cover.**

provoked a flurry of bad press, mostly headlines over his self-confessed addiction to heroin. But, despite warnings from friends and family, Kate continued the relationship. In fact, it seemed that the more warnings she got about Pete, the more irresistible he became to her. Text messages from her to him that were sold to a national newspaper seemed to confirm that she wanted nothing more than to settle down with him. She declared him as 'my only love' and pleaded with him to give up the drugs to live with her in her Cotswold retreat.

But Pete is not the first and probably won't be the last. Kate has made something of a lifestyle out of chasing bad boys. Her previous conquests include Hollywood superstar hell-raiser Jack Nicholson. The actor is infamous for his wild lifestyle and dalliances with hookers and controlled substances. He was twice her age, too – but, in bad-boy years, he's forever young. The supermodel has also been linked to the future James Bond, actor Daniel Craig, wild man Johnny Knoxville and TV presenter and comedian Russell Brand, who is a self-confessed recovering heroin addict himself. Even her great love Johnny Depp was not the family man he is today back when they dated. Kate loved the Johnny who was trashing hotel rooms and owner of one of LA's wildest nightclubs, the Viper Room. It seems that, for Kate, flirting with danger is an essential component of flirting with men.

Despite her hectic lifestyle, and the cocaine scandal, Kate's career has soared. She has just finished shooting a campaign for Rimmel and Virgin and has worked virtually non-stop for labels such as Burberry, Cerruti, Versace, Dolce &

CELEBRITY LIFE LAUNDRY

Gabbana and Chanel. She has a reputation for being highly professional, and was praised in particular by one photographer for her chameleon-like ability to interpret moods instantly. At her peak, Kate earned modelling fees of up to $10,000 a day. Today, this unpretentious girl from Croydon has become an international cultural icon. 'There is something magical about Kate,' says Carine Roitfeld, the editor of French *Vogue*.

'She is incredibly accessible,' says another fashion commentator. 'The way she mixes clothes, the way she puts things together – there is no other like her.'

In 2002, a portrait of Kate by Lucian Freud fetched nearly £4 million at auction. Rather than dressing in couture, Kate posed naked while heavily pregnant. She is nothing if not original.

Analyse this: Kate Moss

Kate was discovered at 14 – a crucial psychological stage. She would have been experiencing the normal angst of teenage development and naturally wanting to break away from the influences of her parents. This is a phase that also involves a young person struggling to find out who she is as a developing woman, wanting to fit in and belong to her peer group, getting interested in boyfriends, and affected by how she sees herself and her body image.

However, Kate had to cope with accelerated development. She was catapulted into the limelight in the role of a sexy young model. This new world would have been exciting by its very nature and the people within it

THE THRILL SEEKER

would have formed an influential part of her peer group.

Kate, it seems, would therefore have had to contend with a psychological double message: 'Grow up fast, but stay young.' For a while, she seemed able to contain herself and maintain high professional standards. By channelling her talents, creativity and ability into her work, she was able to establish an enviable position for herself among the world's supermodels.

If Kate had a propensity towards thrill-seeking behaviour, then the exciting world of modelling would have been very appealing. Add to that mix Kate's young age when she became a model, and she would have had all the active ingredients to stimulate her sensation-seeking nature.

In the world of modelling, this would have made her behaviour appear appropriate and not out of place. But what would happen if this behaviour spilled into her personal life? According to research, there is a type of sensation seeker, characterised by the word 'disinhibition', who shows a willingness to take risks with health and physical wellbeing, and as a result may well end up defying social convention. Kate's drug taking may be part of this desire to reach a physiological high, one that is clearly frowned upon by the majority of the culture, leaving her wide open to mass criticism, as well as potentially putting her own health at risk.

Kate was criticised for the bad boys she dated, the way she behaved, and concerns were expressed over her parenting skills. Ironically, this may have fuelled her thrill-seeking behaviour, ensuring that she never perceived herself as predictable and boring.

CELEBRITY LIFE LAUNDRY

Her accelerated development in her professional life may well have equipped Kate to cope with the business side of her life. But perhaps her bravest step was to reach out and ask for help with her drug problems – a mark of her striving to achieve balance in her personal life as well.

TOM CRUISE – THE CONTROLLED THRILL SEEKER

When Tom Cruise was asked to promote the release of the third instalment of his *Mission: Impossible* franchise, he had big plans. The international superstar kicked off his promotional tour with an action-packed itinerary that would rival any assignment given to his on-screen persona, superspy Ethan Hunt. After jetting into New York, Tom headed across Manhattan by motorcycle, sports car, taxi, subway, speedboat and helicopter, all the while greeting screaming fans along the way.

'Tom has always enjoyed finding new ways to connect with the fans and we're both excited to be sharing the movie with them on this incredible stage,' Paula Wagner, Cruise's producing partner, explained, in the context of Tom's frenetic tour. And that was just the beginning.

Next up on the whirlwind tour was Europe. Tom arrived in Rome twenty minutes after the *M:i:III* press conference had begun, but took time to sign autographs for his devoted fans for three and a half hours. After a packed premiere in London's Leicester Square, the actor headed to Paris, where he thrilled hundreds of fans by touching down in a black helicopter to the *Mission: Impossible* theme song. But the best was yet to come. For

THE THRILL SEEKER

the Japanese launch, Tom went all out. He arrived in a speedboat that was being chased by a helicopter beneath Rainbow Bridge. He also took control of one of Tokyo's famous bullet trains with over 150 film fanatics on board – one premiere that the Japanese won't forget for a while.

Tom also used the many appearances around the globe to speak enthusiastically of his joy at the birth of daughter Suri and his love for actress Katie Holmes. In London, Tom revealed that he had barely slept since the birth of his daughter. 'She breastfeeds and I burp,' he laughed. 'Are you kidding me? I love it. I changed her very first diaper.' While in Tokyo he showed that he was not willing to do anything – even fatherhood – by halves, revealing, 'I always wanted to be a father. I remember my whole life I wanted to be a father. So I'm hoping maybe I have ten children. It was the best Father's Day.'

This kind of charisma and passion is vintage Tom Cruise. In fact, it was Tom's electrifying physical presence and charm that made him the perfect choice for the lead role as a fighter pilot in the 1986 film *Top Gun*. The movie's subsequent success at the box office made Tom a household name, and cemented his position as one of Hollywood's most sought-after leading men. His most famous line from the film – 'I feel the need, the need for speed' – quickly became more than an on-screen mantra: it became his motto for life.

While researching his role as the race-car driver Cole Trickle in *Days of Thunder*, Tom discovered a passion for racing and became adept at driving cars at speeds of 175mph. Skip Barber, who has taught movie stars such as

Paul Newman and Steve McQueen to drive fast cars, said of Tom's determination, 'If he had pushed it any further, he could have been good. He crashed all the time, but we fixed that. We got him to think about patience and make a plan during the race.'

But racing didn't seem to be enough to satisfy the actor's thirst for thrills. When driving at breakneck speeds during the shoot began to bore him, Tom took up skydiving. Crew members watched in amazement one day when the star dropped in to the set – by parachute.

When Tom Cruise and then wife Nicole Kidman celebrated their tenth wedding anniversary, they did not jet off to a faraway island or spend a long evening dining at a five-star restaurant; they spent all night riding the 'Big Shot' roller coaster in Las Vegas. This ride, with freefall drops and speeds of up to 200km/h is not for the weedy. And when the pair attended the hotel Bellagio's opening in Vegas in 1998, Cruise performed a trapeze routine during a backstage visit to the 'O Show'.

Legendary action-movie director John Woo was astounded by Tom's extraordinary physical courage on *M:i-II*. He did all his own stunts, including a white-knuckle motorcycle ride, an epic fight and some hair-raising rock climbing. The film opens with a sequence featuring Tom dangling 1,500ft above a canyon, and deftly leaping from one rock face to another. Although the props crew had come up with a fake cliff for the star, Tom insisted on dangling on the real thing. John Woo said at the time, 'He didn't want us to hold the safety cable tight, and he did it seven times. I couldn't watch – not even on the monitor.'

THE THRILL SEEKER

And despite intense training for his role as a hardened warrior in 2003's *The Last Samurai*, Tom nearly had his neck chopped with a samurai sword more than once during filming.

He has come a long way from his nomadic childhood (his father, an engineer, moved the family around constantly). Tom went from school to school and, as soon as he made friends, he quickly had to say goodbye. His taste for thrills began at an early age. 'I was three,' Cruise has said, 'and my mother had left me and my sister in the car while she got some groceries.' When she walked out of the store, she found young Tom behind the wheel, backing the family car into the street. 'Mom dropped the milk, yanked open the door, shoved me out of the seat and stopped the car.'

In a candid interview with *Parade* magazine in April 2006, Tom opened up about his difficult childhood. 'I had no really close friend, I was always the new kid with the wrong shoes, the wrong accent. I didn't have the friend to share things with and confide in.' Tom also talked about his volatile relationship with his father. 'He was a bully and a coward,' he frankly admitted. 'He was the person where, if something goes wrong, they kick you. It was a great lesson in my life – how he'd lull you in, make you feel safe and then, bang!' he revealed. 'For me it was like, "There's something wrong with this guy. Don't trust him. Be careful around him." There's that anxiety.' Despite their turbulent relationship, Tom did see his dad one last time – following a ten-year estrangement – while he was terminally ill. 'He was in the hospital dying of cancer, and he would only meet me on the basis that I didn't ask him anything about the past,' Tom recalled. 'When I saw him in pain, I thought, "What a lonely life." He was in his late forties. It was sad.'

Tom's battle with dyslexia was a difficult part of his childhood. 'The school took me to a psychiatrist to get tested,' he once recalled. 'They said, "Oh, he's dyslexic." I'm labelled. It instantly put me into confusion. It was an absolute affront to my dignity.' In fact, the diagnosis only made him determined to get to the bottom of the condition. 'I remember thinking, "I've got to figure this out. What's normal? Am I normal? Who's to say what's normal?" I didn't understand what "normal" is. It still doesn't make sense.'

While Tom struggled with school and his dyslexia, he also faced the difficult task of adjusting to his parents' divorce, which happened when he was just 11 years old. It was a tough time for Tom, but by the time he was 14 his family finally settled in New Jersey, and life began to improve for the future star. He threw himself into sports, wrestling being his particular passion. He was very successful until a serious knee injury prevented him from further competition. A role in the senior-class production of *Guys and Dolls* ignited his spark for acting, and, within five short months of leaving school and moving to pursue acting in New York, Tom Cruise hit the big screen.

Since then, virtually nothing has stopped him from attacking life like a man possessed. Tom has said he gets by on no more than five hours' sleep a night, and in his spare time likes to run, sail, fly planes, sky dive, do gymnastics, scuba dive and roller blade.

The diversity of the roles Tom has chosen also reveals his

THE THRILL SEEKER

love of risk. He has never been content with just playing the likeable sex-symbol hero of *Top Gun*, *Mission: Impossible* and *War of the Worlds*. He played a disabled Vietnam veteran in *Born on the Fourth of July*, an erotically charged vampire in *Interview with the Vampire*, and more recently a grey-haired cold-blooded killer in *Collateral*.

Tom's public image and privacy remained one area in which he seemed to take virtually no risks at all. He employed Pat Kingsley, one of Hollywood's most feared and powerful publicists, who maintained tight control of what was written and said about the megastar. Those seeking an interview had to submit questions beforehand, and sign contracts swearing to stay away from certain subjects that were strictly off-limits. Tom sued frequently to correct stories about him that he said were untrue, and

---

While filming *Mission Impossible: III*, Tom Cruise terrified producers by insisting on carrying out his own death-defying stunts. The actor has reportedly refused to allow a stunt double to do the dangerous high falls necessary for his part as secret agent Ethan Hunt in the sequel. His willingness to push himself to the limit is said to have worried stunt co-ordinator Vic Armstrong, who is working on the film with him. According to Vic, 'He did a 70ft fall for us last week. He's amazing, he did about seven takes. Absolutely terrifies me – I can see the headlines. What a way to finish a career.'

Total Film **magazine, November 2005**

gained a reputation as one of Hollywood's most litigious celebrities. While he jumped out of planes in his personal life, he never took chances with reporters. Until now.

In 2005, Tom caused shock waves when he fired Kingsley, and hired his sister to handle his PR. Shortly afterwards, the 43-year-old actor began publicly dating 27-year-old *Dawson's Creek* actress Katie Holmes. In a moment of stunning candour on *Oprah*, when the chat-show hostess remarked upon how happy the star seemed, he gushed, 'I'm in love.' Tom then proceeded to jump up on Oprah's couch, excitedly waving his arms in the air.

The couple was quickly dubbed 'Tomkat' by the press, and newspapers and magazines all over the globe showed them kissing and cuddling like a pair of amorous teenagers. Tom even announced their engagement during a press conference. This was a very different Tom Cruise to the one the media had been used to.

Tom is also becoming more frank and outspoken about his faith. A devout advocate of Scientology, he has become the church's most famous ambassador. He has opened Scientology centres around the world and, to the amazement of cast and crew, he even had a Scientology tent erected near the set of the 2005 blockbuster *War of the Worlds*. In accordance with his beliefs, Tom has also publicly lobbied against the use of anti-depressants to treat post-natal depression.

As Tom continues to seek thrills with unstoppable determination, he remains one of the world's biggest box-office draws – he has already won three Golden Globes, had three Academy Award nominations and starred in over

THE THRILL SEEKER

30 films. Well into his forties, his appetite for risk and life in the fast lane continues unabated, and this character trait has made him astronomically successful. He has taken risks with his roles to show his talent, and his physical efforts have turned a host of legendary directors into his biggest fans. Those who have worked with Tom say that there is something about his thirst for excitement that makes him light up the screen with irresistible energy even when not in the middle of acrobatic fight scenes, roaring car chases or shoot-outs. He has managed to channel his thirst for thrills creatively, and has become a Hollywood legend as a result.

Analyse this: Tom Cruise
Tom Cruise certainly appears to have had early thrill-seeking tendencies, starting when as a three-year-old he released the handbrake of his mother's car. But Tom's nomadic early childhood may also have had a lasting effect on his perception of relationships as being quick and short term.

A child like Tom, who moved through a succession of schools, would have had to develop an extraordinary ability to develop friendships very quickly, as a means of survival, before his family upped sticks and moved again. This may have made him adept at negotiating the early stages of friendships, but perhaps also unsure of how to maintain them, and deepen relationships, once this initial stage was over. Having to deal with his parents' divorce would have further cemented his feeling that relationships are merely temporary arrangements. And having to manage his dyslexia would have brought its own psychological burden. This may well have affected his perception of himself, and brought out other emotions, including anger, frustration and feeling at odds with himself – emotions that, according to research, often accompany dyslexia.

As an adult, his desire for thrill-seeking pursuits became more apparent, placing him in high-risk situations. There appears to be a compulsion in him to achieve the ultimate thrill. Through his work as an actor, he could have his cake and eat it; he could act out a wide range of roles and be quite safe. Or so you'd think. But no. Quite the opposite.

And, significantly, Tom's adult behaviour in relationships appears to mirror his early experiences with the ability to form powerful emotional bonds very quickly. Unsurprisingly this has led to marriage, divorce and marriage again. Perhaps Thrill Seekers find the early stages of love, romance and the increased pulse rate that it brings highly intoxicating.

Being very controlled in certain areas of his life may also echo early experiences, in this case his father's unpredictable behaviour, leaving the young Tom unsure of what mood his father could be in. Remember, Tom himself described his father as a 'coward and a bully'.

It's possible that being controlled may also have a positive side effect, enabling Tom to regulate his thrill-seeking impulses. However, when we see him showing his thrill-seeking side on *Oprah*, for instance, what comes over strongly is the very childlike and impulsive nature of the Thrill Seeker and how, in the wrong context, it can seem chaotic and reckless.

THE THRILL SEEKER

NOW ABOUT YOU

Find out: are you an extreme Thrill Seeker?

Take a moment to read each question carefully. (If in doubt, make your best guess, and try not to leave questions unanswered.) If you answer affirmatively to more than four of them, the answer to the question above may be 'Yes'.

1. Do you sometimes like to do things that are a little bit frightening?
2. Are you impulsive and prone to taking risks?
3. Do you get impatient with people you consider to be dull or boring?
4. Do you prefer friends who are exciting and unpredictable?
5. Do you like to live 'in the moment', without worrying about the consequences?
6. Do you find that rules and regulations hem you in?
7. Were you brought up in a highly charged household?
8. Are you restless and twitchy if you stay at home on your own for any length of time?

WHY AM I AN EXTREME THRILL SEEKER?

There are several possible explanations. Let's look at three key factors.

Genes

There is a significant body of research that points to a thrill-seeking gene. In a study published in the *American Journal of Genetics* at UCLA, researchers announced that they had found two types of mutant genes that play a role in causing and maintaining personality traits leading to thrill-seeking behaviours. Current research indicates that about 30 per cent of the population has one of these genes, and 20 per cent has both.

Environment

This too is an important developmental factor, helping to shape how a person reacts to situations, manages his or her emotions and develops an understanding of rules and boundaries.

For example, if you attended many different schools because your parents kept switching jobs, moving from area to area, you'd have become used to making new friends, only to find you had to move on again. If you stayed at any school for longer than normal, you may have then found it difficult to settle because you were actually waiting to move and start afresh. In order to get that buzz of moving, you might have started to 'play up' at school and react badly to rules. And your parents, who may have felt guilty about the constant moves, might not therefore have contained or dealt with your bad behaviour. Not being taught how to your control impulses, or contain excitation appropriately, could potentially lead to high risk taking and even antisocial behaviour.

THE THRILL SEEKER

Evolution

At one time in human history, thrill seeking was a distinct advantage. It enabled individuals to seek out new territory for the tribe, or work out which foods were safe and which were poisonous. But in our modern world, thrill seeking that isn't channelled in a socially acceptable way – and when combined with other risk factors like high degree of impulsiveness, an absence of fear and a reliance on the adrenaline buzz – can be dangerous.

THE POSITIVES AND NEGATIVES

Thrill seeking can be a wonderful gift, enabling you to lead an active life, being confident enough to take risks and able to make things happen. You live life to its fullest, positive that you will prevail. However, being a Thrill Seeker can cause problems. You might be taking too many impulsive and life-threatening risks. If this is you, being driven by impulse and getting a rush from an adrenaline high, you may have done some things – quite dangerous things – that now amaze you. No wonder that others didn't follow you, and you ended up calling them boring.

So let's look at the following case history using the CBT model, and see how beliefs affect thoughts, feelings and behaviour.

Jane was at a party with some new acquaintances. She was having a great time. During the course of the evening, one of her new friends offered her some recreational drugs, claiming that she'd get the ultimate high from them. This completely appealed to her and, without thinking twice, she went for it, undeterred by the consequences. She woke up the next morning in a stranger's bed next to a guy she didn't recognise, and wondering what on earth had happened the night before.

The result? The need for excitement had put her in a potentially dangerous situation. She may have got her adrenaline kick from doing something she perceived as novel and exciting, but at the same time she risked her health and safety.

What should I do if I'm like Jane?
The healthy response involves…

1. Understanding your attitudes so that you recognise your emotional triggers, meaning you're more in control.
2. Taking a step back from the situation so that you can consider the consequences of your actions. This will help you to think before you act.
3. Changing the way you approach new situations, assessing the risks to yourself and reducing the risk of impulsive actions.
4. Taking steps so that your thrill seeking isn't a major problem.

THE NEED TO SLOW DOWN

Now consider the following case history. Sarah was away for the weekend with some friends. She planned the

THE THRILL SEEKER

whole thing – camping in the woods, swimming in rivers, the lot. She was really excited about going back to nature, and the thrill of what could happen out there in the dark really got her going.

While on the trip, she suggested a midnight walk. A few friends were up for it, but the rest told her she was crazy, and decided to stay behind. On the walk, she found a riverbank and wanted to jump into the water to see how deep it was. Before anyone could stop her, she'd gone headlong into the depths. The water was freezing, but that didn't bother her. She was excited and felt alive. She yelled to the others to follow her, but they refused.

What should I do if I'm like Sarah?

As Daniel Goleman suggests in his book *Emotional Intelligence*, we have two minds – a rational and an emotional one – and they usually work in harmony: 'But when passions surge, the balance tips: it is the emotional mind that captures the upper hand, swamping the rational mind.' In other words, there is a strong temptation to lose yourself in the moment and forget the consequences. Thriving on adventure is like being a moth to a flame. Throwing yourself into the river is dangerously reckless but the big question is, how can you slow down? By training yourself to focus on the consequences.

One quick, simple and highly effective exercise is to count to 20 slowly, while concentrating on breathing in and then out. It also gives you time to switch on rationally and decide on alternative ways of behaving.

GAIN INSIGHT

You may have inherited your sensation-seeking nature, and had this compounded by a highly charged environment where raising the pulse rate and getting an adrenaline rush was the norm, so much so that it became a way of life. You may therefore keep trying to recreate these feelings to feel completely alive. If that's the case, every time you start doing something potentially dangerous, say to yourself something along the lines of: 'Where does this idea come from? And is the emotional sensation and buzz worth risking my safety?' You have to challenge yourself. Use the diary exercise from Chapter 1 (page xx) to identify your moods, and notice how they affect your thinking and behaviour. This will enable you to identify, challenge and then break potentially harmful attitudes.

As Goleman comments in *Emotional Intelligence*, 'There is perhaps no psychological skill more fundamental than resisting impulse. It is the root of all emotional self-control, since all emotions, by their very nature, lead to one or another impulse to act.'

> **CELEBRITY TIP**
> Angelina Jolie has managed to successfully channel her thrill-seeking energies into awareness-raising charity work. She has confidently and constructively used her abilities to travel to

THE THRILL SEEKER

dangerous places in the world and try to make a difference to the lives of those less fortunate.

Like Angelina, plan your buzz. You can still get excitement by being careful and taking time to plan your adventure. Channel your thrill-seeking side so that no one is put at risk. Try planned adventurous pursuits like mountaineering, or white-water rafting that will necessitate training from qualified professionals to eliminate any danger.

HOW THRILL SEEKERS LOVE THESE ARE THE KEY MODES:

Excitement
You love the thrill of the chase and, no matter how many times you get rebuffed, you keep going back for more. But the moment your interest is reciprocated, you get bored and become withdrawn and distant. Yet going from one person to the next leaves you unfulfilled. You get restless and look for the next adventure, and are almost too willing to dispense with lovers, blaming them for losing their spark.

Birds of a feather
You may have been attracted to someone just like you – adventurous, exciting and daring. The problem was, you could never rein each other in, and at times things got out

of hand. The compatible relationship may have ended because neither of you knew where to establish the boundaries, and pushed each other to the limits instead.

In other words, being driven by adrenaline can mean that you are more interested in the buzz than the person. You may avoid closeness in intimate relationships because this makes you restless. You may be so focused on raising your heart rate that you forget that there are two of you in the relationship. Instead of self-reflection, you may find yourself blaming the other person for not being exciting enough.

THE HEALTHY RELATIONSHIP FOR YOU

Being a Thrill Seeker is very exciting, and has wonderful strengths, but also has its problems. If you think you're a Thrill Seeker, then…

1. Learn to take a step back, and recognise how your behaviour affects those closest to you, instead of imposing your wishes on them.
2. Choose a potential partner who enables you to express your high energy levels, but who also challenges you to think before you act.
3. Channel your energies and abilities into positive areas in your work and spare time.

In short, by learning to be with someone who can contain you and also let you grow, you'll realise that a relationship can be long term and still exciting. That's the one for you.

4
The Natural Talent

Everything you tackle seems to turn to gold. The parties you organise are a great success, and at work you are clearly an achiever. But are you constantly afraid of how others perceive you? Do you ever feel crippled by self-doubt, despite your success?

We're calling this personality type the 'Natural Talent'. The psychological characteristics of the Natural Talent as outlined here are based on research by psychology professor Pauline Ross Clance and psychotherapist Suzanne Imes, who called it the 'impostor phenomenon'. They conducted a study of more than 150 high-achieving women, and identified five common themes. Each Natural Talent person...

> 1. Has a persistent belief in their lack of competence, skill or intelligence, despite plenty of evidence to the contrary.
> 2. Identifies achievement as being down to luck, fate and attractiveness – not ability.
> 3. Believes that they have manipulated people's impressions of them.

THE NATURAL TALENT

4. Believes that they are undeserving, and have tricked people into thinking otherwise.
5. Has the tendency to play up their weaknesses and play down their strengths.

In short, people who share this personality type may have tendencies towards depression, anxiety, fear of failure and fears that they will be exposed as a fraud. This, in turn, may result in feelings of shame and low self-esteem. And, surprisingly, research estimates that about 30 per cent of the population – both men and women – demonstrates some form of this thinking.

We've selected the following three extraordinary and successful celebrities because they are balanced examples of individuals who exhibit some of these characteristics, but in their most healthy state – based on what we know about them in the public arena. A balanced type of Natural Talent plays to his or her strengths and has an awareness of how to manage difficult situations. Nicole Kidman, Jennifer Aniston and Robbie Williams manage their lives in ways that have brought them tremendous success. The downside, however, is that if you become an extreme of this type you might well suffer from feelings of depression and anxiety.

NICOLE KIDMAN – THE RELUCTANT NATURAL TALENT

Walking down an aisle that looked like a runway of roses and candles at a cliff-top chapel in Sydney, Australia, Nicole Kidman was wiping away tears of joy. Standing at the end of the candlelit aisle was the man she hoped to spend the rest of her life with, country music heartthrob Keith Urban. After heartfelt vows during a romantic ceremony in which both were moved to tears, Keith serenaded his bride at the star-studded reception and pledged that, 'I will love you forever... I will be your rock and refuge' in front of more than 200 family and friends. As Nicole's eyes welled yet again with tears, her new husband went on to declare loudly that his love for her would last until the end of time, at which point the room erupted in cheers. 'He said he knew she'd had some hard times but he was here now – her rock,' an insider revealed.

It was exactly the kind of thing that Nicole needed to hear.

The truth is, Nicole Kidman has never found fame easy. Despite universal acclaim from film critics and fashion pundits, the stunning Aussie star has freely admitted to struggling with being a celebrity. She often suffers from insomnia and has admitted in the press to suffering panic attacks at film premieres. In April 2002, Nicole told *Vogue* that she regularly suffers from such attacks when surrounded by cameras: 'My hands start shaking and I have trouble breathing... Tom would always whisper to me that everything was all right.'

While married to former husband Tom Cruise, Nicole relied heavily on him to hold her hand and offer support during red-carpet press line-ups. After the split, Nicole almost always arrived with one of her close circle of female friends and family.

Despite being one of the world's great actresses, Nicole

THE NATURAL TALENT

seems to lack confidence. After accepting a role, she sometimes feels certain that she won't be able to do it. She has admitted in the past that, 'I always have doubts – on everything.' In a curious way, she finds that these insecurities motivate her, as she considers it arrogant to be too confident about an acting job. Surprisingly, winning an Academy Award in 2003 did not help. Nicole revealed that her victory did not even register for about a year. Finally, after being introduced at a public event as 'Oscar-winner Nicole Kidman', she began to believe it. Still she felt no joy; on the contrary, 'That's when I got embarrassed.' She confessed, 'I was afraid that every time I walked on a set after that, people were going to expect me to be really good.'

She has spoken openly of her deep and crippling depression following her divorce from Tom Cruise. At one stage, she acknowledged that she found it impossible to get dressed and fix her hair, and that she stayed in her pyjamas for weeks at a time. Since the breakdown of her marriage, Nicole's private life has been fodder for gossip columns. She has been linked with a number of men, including singer Lenny Kravitz, New Zealand businessman Eric Watson, Elizabeth Hurley's ex Steve Bing, and most recently fellow Aussie and country music star Keith Urban. Nicole has strong feelings about what she wants in a man: 'I like to be able to express myself, but I'm a woman so I also like to be taken care of. I like the feeling of somebody who's by your side who will stand up for you, help you, protect you and be there for you in the long run.'

CELEBRITY LIFE LAUNDRY

> Screen goddess Nicole Kidman gets so nervous on the red carpet that her hands turn beet red, according to eyewitnesses. The actress has made no secret of her trepidation at public events and, while she is often able to control shaking hands, there is no way to prevent her palms from turning scarlet. At the New York premiere of her film *Birth*, many in the media commented on her beet-red palms, in sharp contrast to the rest of her milky-white complexion. 'It's a nervous reaction,' says one source. 'She is aware of it but can do nothing about it.'
>
> And with her lack of confidence, it's no wonder she's scared. 'I'm always shocked when people go to see my movies,' the actress has said, 'I still don't understand how any of this happened. This is not something I ever sought. I never went after the brass ring. I just wanted to be a working actress.'

Her private life is carefully guarded. She has, however, poured her heart out to her friends, including Oscar-winner Sean Penn, with whom she co-starred in *The Interpreter*. In 2005, Penn was quoted in the *Daily Telegraph* as saying that Nicole has 'an intense relationship with disappointment'. Maybe that's why Nicole surrounds herself with a strong support system. She has maintained close friendships with people she has known for most of her life. 'The most important thing is the people you have your friendships with, and who are

THE NATURAL TALENT

going to be there through your whole life,' she says. 'I've got friends that I've known since I was born and we look at each other and go, "Can you believe we're still here?" My sister Antonia is my other half, and I have a number of girlfriends. Naomi Watts and I are very good friends and have maintained that through so many things. I think that's really rare, particularly for actresses, and I take a lot of pride in that.'

Nicole tries to keep away from prying eyes. While at home with her family in Sydney, friends say the actress lives a somewhat reclusive life – a result of being regularly hounded by the paparazzi, one of whom was caught recently trying to bug her home. She also covers up – while swimming, she wears a wetsuit, goggles and swim cap, and if jogging she dons a full-length black tracksuit, baseball cap and sunglasses

As for her social life, Nicole is hardly an avid party-goer. She often has dinner with friends, and seems to prefer being in her own home or at a friend's house. Her holidays are based on seclusion – she spends time on a private Fijian island, visits her family in Australia or stays at a friend's villa in Italy. It's ironic that someone who appears to hate the limelight so much should have sought out a career that has placed her so firmly in the centre of it. 'I just can't believe that I'm even in a position to be making movies, to be honest,' she revealed on CBS's news programme *The Early Show*, in October 2004. 'There's times when I go, "I can't believe somebody wants me to be in their movie."'

CELEBRITY LIFE LAUNDRY

Analyse this: Nicole Kidman

Nicole certainly appears to evince characteristics of the Natural Talent. This may mean that, whatever she achieves, she may put down at some deep level to luck or a mistake. Someone with these tendencies worries that they are going to be revealed as a fraud, and one who has deceived everyone for a long time. But with Nicole there appears to be a double message. On the one hand, she may feel a fraud, yet on the other she may also be quite aware of her own talent and potential.

So it's not surprising that Nicole can be thrust into the limelight in a wide array of acting roles, and give amazing performances in them, while the simple act of walking down a red carpet, and just being herself, could cause her anguish.

This double message is played out many times in what she does. On the one hand, there is a possibility she has potentially crippling self-doubts when offered a role, trying to convince the director that he has made a mistake in choosing her (a classic Natural Talent tendency). But, by accepting such roles, she is then able to showcase her extraordinary talents and receive justifiably high praise.

ROBBIE WILLIAMS – THE OUTRAGEOUS NATURAL TALENT

Amid fireworks and loud cheers, in June 2006 Robbie Williams took to the stage in Dublin for the opening night of his summer tour. As 78,000 fans screamed, Robbie kicked off his storming stage show and sent the

THE NATURAL TALENT

assembled masses into delirium. However, while the crowd rose to frenzied levels after his third track, 'Tripping', the singing superstar abruptly stopped in order to catch his breath – and have a cup of tea! Addressing the gathered thousands, he declared, 'It's been too long. I don't know how Mick Jagger does this. I'm knackered!'

The fans loved his concert and excitement reached a fever pitch when he began the show's final song, 'Let Me Entertain You', during which Robbie was set to drop almost 100ft to the stage in a 'gondola'. However, an unfortunate technical glitch occurred backstage, and the stunt had to be abandoned. Robbie ended up running on to the set in a panic as fire exploded around him. While some performers may have laughed it off, or even pretended that it was all part of the show, a clearly shocked and fuming Robbie told the crowd, 'I can let you into a little secret. When I was up there I was supposed to come down in a gondola and it was going to be entertainment at its highest peak. But when the man standing behind you says, "It's fucked" in front of 70,000 people, you panic. Being in a white tracksuit probably wasn't the best thing to be in. You'll never know how much panic went through my mind when I was up there. You've been much better than me. I've not been very good tonight so I will come back and do it for free.'

Robbie Williams has it all. He is handsome, successful, famous and, in his own words, 'rich beyond my wildest dreams!' His record sales top 40 million, he owns million-pound homes in London and Los Angeles, and he continues to win rave reviews on each new project.

CELEBRITY LIFE LAUNDRY

Despite his great success, however, the music megastar has admitted to feeling depressed, unhappy and insecure.

Robbie Williams shocked his fans when he cancelled the Asian leg of his 2006 world tour. As pals close to the star expressed concern about his health, Robbie admitted that he sometimes suffers from depression and that he was exhausted. Robbie's Close Encounters tour was supposed to include gigs at Shanghai, Bangkok, Hong Kong and Singapore. A brief statement from his management revealed: 'It became clear that the stress and exhaustion from the Asian tour coming shortly after the end of the European dates would seriously impact his health.' According to one report, the signs of fatigue were there when Robbie performed at Milton Keynes shortly before his decision. The star was said to be sweating profusely and telling the 65,000 fans he 'felt like shit'. One fan said, 'He seemed out of control, you could see it all on the big screen.' Another said, 'He just wasn't himself. He couldn't stop sweating.'

He is a recovering drug and alcohol addict, has yet to find lasting love and has failed to break into the one market – America – that would cement his position as king of the crooners. The singer has admitted to suffering bouts of insomnia in the past, saying, 'I can't get to sleep nowadays until five in the morning. It used to be much easier with alcohol.'

So what's keeping him awake? It seems that Robbie is not entirely sure he deserves his stardom. 'By rights I should be in Stoke-on-Trent in some pub right now talking about how I used to sing when I was a kid. I

THE NATURAL TALENT

shouldn't be a famous pop star. However, I do work bloody hard and I'm bloody good at it so I do probably deserve it after all.' Probably? It seems that, no matter how much success he finds, Robbie Williams doesn't seem to be able to shake the feeling that all of his fame may have been down to chance – a freak stroke of good fortune that could run out at any second. He may feel that, sooner or later, his fans will find someone else to worship and all the fun will be over.

Robbie's desire to please everyone seems evident in his professional choices. A quick glance at his career shows that the only consistent thing is his lack of consistency. Over the course of five albums, he has swung wildly from the bold confidence of debut album *Life Thru a Lens* to the Rat Pack overtones of his second LP, *I've Been Expecting You*, to the jazz-crooner style that characterises *Swing When You're Winning*. As he has said, 'I want to be like David Bowie or Iggy Pop, but I'm more like Norman Wisdom.' This all-over-the-map approach seems to epitomise Robbie's desire to find success in every arena.

And what about the private Robbie Williams? One article in the *Observer* from October 2005 described him as 'extremely sharp and uncommonly warm when he wants to be; he is always alert and yet somehow constantly bored'. So you begin to wonder what lies beneath the self-generated press, the outrageous antics and bold hyperbole. Although he seems to enjoy being the perennial bachelor, he is quoted as saying his true desire is to settle down and have a family.

CELEBRITY LIFE LAUNDRY

Robbie has been linked to a trail of stunning women, including the model Rachel Hunter, actress Anna Friel, pop star Nicole Appleton and Jimmy Choo shoes boss Tamara Mellon. And yet, in a 2005 interview, Robbie admitted that he had never been in love. 'I've had a giant expectation. I wake up every morning with fucking expectations. But I've never had a love in the sense that other people have experienced it. No one's ever – and I don't think it's anybody's fault other than mine – fallen in love with me that way.' Robbie's desire to be universally appreciated also seems to affect his sex life. He teases both sexes with outrageous comments, recently saying that what he'd like very much is to 'experience the female orgasm'. As one reporter put it, he is 'very good at appearing as if he lives in some sort of outer-sexual hinterland where anyone is game, so long as they adore him'.

> **Robbie Williams says he's not worried about being single, insisting he isn't lonely because he gets everything he needs from sleeping pills and his computer. The singer regularly types his name into internet search engine Google to see what people are saying about him. He says, 'Look, we could all psychoanalyse Robbie Williams. I'm not desperate to be in a relationship. It's another piece of the jigsaw, that's all. I'm alone. I'm not lonely. I'm OK. I've got the computer and the sleeping pills. Things are fine. I know people will say, "Check out the ego on Robbie**

THE NATURAL TALENT

Williams going online to see what people say about him." But it's never anything nice!'

His latest album, *Intensive Care*, was Robbie's biggest seller ever and, to top it off, he recently sold 1.6 million concert tickets in one day. 'That's a world record,' Williams says of his ticket sales. 'But that was the peak right there. You can't get any better than that. So you're speaking to a man on the decline.' However, being on stage, Robbie is often plagued by self-doubt. 'I find it a tremendous responsibility. For me it's not like, "One, two, three… rock'n'roll star." For me it's like, "Oh, God, here's an hour and fifty where I've got to be on stage." People have come to expect a certain level of entertainment, what I expect of myself is complete exhaustion every time I go on stage. They've paid money to come and see me, I'm going to give them the show they expect. I'm working my bollocks off up there. Now, whether I enjoy it is nobody else's business.'

Despite being an enormous hit in the charts and with the ladies, Robbie admits that he is so shy and fragile that the swagger and confidence so evident on stage vanishes when he goes home. 'I'm like a balloon. If you stick a pin in me I would just pop,' he said. 'If I went out there and the audience didn't like me, I would crumble.'

CELEBRITY LIFE LAUNDRY

Born in 1974 in Stoke-on-Trent, from an early age, Robbie revealed himself as a natural entertainer with a thirst for fame. His father Peter was a singer and entertainer who toured the northern club circuit, so as a boy Robbie was effectively raised by his mother Janet and an older sister Sally. A class clown at school, Robbie always seemed destined for something bigger. As he told one reporter, 'You'll do anything for your 15 minutes of fame. Dead right. I'd have signed any contract, I'd have climbed the Eiffel Tower in my Y-fronts with "Shit on me, seagulls" written on my back.'

Fortunately for Robbie, he didn't have to. After an early role on TV's *Brookside*, his big break came when he became part of boy band Take That. He was famous by the age of 15.

Robbie's struggle with substances has been well documented and, when he became strictly sober five years ago, he had to find alternative outlets for his compulsive nature. As he admits, 'I am a split personality, a psychiatrist's dream – and I've been to a few of them.' He admits to occasionally finding the knocks he gets from critics hard to take, though. He told one reporter, 'What happens is I speak to people outside of my circle of friends and they have already formed an opinion of me based on the things that people have written. That is the effect of journalism on my life and sometimes it isn't very pleasant… I'm just not in the fucking place for this shit to drop off me. I'm not Buddha. I'm fucking 31, still human, you know.'

Robbie has been philosophical about his success. 'When you're 13, 14, 15 and you've got your Walkman

THE NATURAL TALENT

on and you're walking through Piccadilly Gardens in Manchester or you're at the bus station in Stoke and it's raining, then the possibility of being exactly who you want to be is at its strongest. Your expectation is of sex and of drinking and taking your first E, or maybe being on the TV or in a loving relationship, and the expectation of all of that stuff is just so beautiful and perfect.' At the same time, he acknowledges that this sounds very sad: 'Yes, because you know the punch line to it. Because you know that the reality of all that stuff is not quite so beautiful. It's messy and addictive and fucked up. Killing the expectation – or maybe just letting it go gently – is the best thing that I can do with it.'

Analyse this: Robbie Williams

Robbie has the key ingredients for a person with Natural Talent tendencies. On the outside, he seems to be a winning combination of self-deprecation and arrogance. He is driven to achieve, and is certainly not afraid to be in the spotlight. But underneath it all he appears to be afflicted by nagging doubts that he will be exposed as a fake. There is a strong underlying message of 'I don't deserve it' in what he says about himself. Perhaps the self-deprecation is not solely an act.

Psychologically, he seems to find it very difficult to reconcile public success with private feelings of being a fraud. There is a constant tension between his achievement-orientated self – and he has clearly worked very hard, driven by the hunger first to achieve and then to maintain his fame – and doubts about his ability. This makes for a very uncomfortable state of mind, and perhaps unsurprisingly may have led to the use of drink and drugs to drown out the conflicting emotions.

He also, classically, suffers from the pressure not to fail. This may be most strongly connected to the desire to avoid being found out, and sadly means that he may have real difficulty in enjoying the fruits of his labour. There appears to be considerable confusion in the context of his relationships, too. Who am I? What do I want, and from whom? In many ways, he is simultaneously 'everyman' and 'no man'. This has given him mass appeal, but perhaps has left him at times unsure and unclear as to who he really is.

JENNIFER ANISTON – THE EMOTIONAL NATURAL TALENT

'I've had moments of insecurity in my life. I've had moments of low self-esteem. I think it's something that's universal that everyone feels. Just because you get put on top of a wedding cake, which is not your choice, or you've been given this image doesn't mean it's who you are or what you believe.' Jennifer Aniston

It was a quiet morning in April 2005 when Jennifer Aniston got a phone call that sent her reeling. It was a friend, telling her that photographs had been published of her husband Brad Pitt on vacation with his new girlfriend, Angelina Jolie. The two were frolicking on a beach in Kenya, with Angelina's little boy Maddox next to them, building sandcastles. 'The world was shocked, and I was shocked,' Jennifer later admitted. 'Who would deal with that and say, "Isn't that sweet! That looks like fun!" But shit happens. You joke and say, "What doesn't kill you makes you stronger." Am I lonely? Yes. Do I have my days when I've thrown a little pity party for myself? Absolutely.' Although she added, 'I'm also doing really well,' things quickly got harder for her when it emerged that Angelina had given birth to Brad's little girl amid a blaze of publicity. Asked recently about her feelings on her divorce, Jen denied any bitterness. 'I don't regret any of that time and I'm not here to beat myself up about it,' she told the *News of the World*. 'They were seven very intense years together and it was a beautiful, complicated relationship. I will love Brad for the rest of my life and I hope that some day we will be able to be friends again.'

Whatever Jen felt at the time of her public split, it did not keep her from doing her job. In fact, immediately following the break-up, she threw herself into her work, shooting four movies in a row. According to those on set, Jen was positive, warm and kind to all. *Rumour Has It* set decorator Jay Hart recalls that the actress remained remarkably professional despite her public-private trauma. 'There was no evidence of emotion other than about the work,' he said.

She was similarly poised during the *Friends with Money* shoot in winter 2005. 'She arrived right in the middle of that crazy maelstrom of her private life,' says her co-star Jason Isaacs, adding, 'She was so professional and focused and lovely.'

CELEBRITY LIFE LAUNDRY

Despite the professional veneer, Jennifer has been open about how she gets her feelings hurt. After reading a magazine interview in which Rod Stewart's daughter Kimberly said she liked Jen 'because she's homely. She obviously has to have something else – it's not like she's gorgeous or anything,' Jen confessed, 'It literally ruined my night. I got my feelings very hurt, actually.'

Although admittedly a sensitive person, Jen no longer reads newspapers or gossip magazines in which she may read something about herself. 'I don't read it and I don't look at it,' she says. 'It's actually easier than you think… I don't live in a city where I'm walking by newsstands… I'm in a car driving by them… I just don't pay attention. It's also the rule among my friends and family.'

In order to reduce the glare of excess tabloid attention, nowadays Jen is tight-lipped about romantic relationships. When asked about her reported affair with her *Break-Up* co-star Vince Vaughn, she refused to answer, or even to confirm they were a couple. And, despite paparazzi shots of the couple cruising on the Seine and holding hands at a Chicago Cubs baseball game, they refused point blank to pose next to each other for photographers at any of their film's many premieres.

As for her current state of mind, Jen says she's healed and moved on. 'I've gone for each type of man. The rough guy, the nerdy, sweet, lovable type, the slick guy. Men in general are a good thing, I think… In a man, I look for a friend, someone who is an equal and with whom I'm comfortable… I want to be loved, happy and not settle for something less than we all deserve.'

THE NATURAL TALENT

Jennifer Aniston told one interviewer that she has been dogged by 'low self-esteem' and 'a sense of shame', putting much of the turmoil in her life down to a bitter rift with her mother Nancy, a former model. She says, 'This is my last chunk of disease in my life – my mom.' They have not spoken in four years and Aniston snubbed her mother, not inviting her to her wedding on a Malibu clifftop, which she described as a 'tortuous decision'. Of her years growing up with her mother, she says, 'I don't know if I would have known how beautiful she was if she wasn't always pointing out how unbeautiful I was.'

Vanity Fair, May 2001

'Marriage brings up all the things I pushed to the back-burner – the fears, the mistrust, the doubts, the insecurities. It's like opening Pandora's box. Every question comes out.' Insecurities about her looks are a common theme: 'I think I'm just starting to feel I can stop apologising – to myself, to my family, to my friends, to the world – and live in my body and be OK with that.' Jennifer immediately regretted cutting her hair at one stage: 'I did it mainly to relieve me of the bondage of self,' she says. 'It was the right time to do it – shed the skin – but I couldn't hate it more. It's just not me. I hide behind my hair, it's my shield. I'm taking every horse vitamin there is to make it grow faster – blue-green algae, you name it.'

Vanity Fair, May 2001

Jennifer grew up as the only daughter of an actor dad, soap star John Aniston, and an ex model mum. She spent her childhood moving around frequently, bouncing from a tiny home in Sherman Oaks, California, to a Manhattan apartment. Although her parents moved in Hollywood circles – the actor Telly Savalas was her godfather – money was usually short. The family even spent a year living with her grandmother in Athens, Greece.

Worse, Jennifer's mother often criticised her looks as a child, telling her that her nose was too big and her eyes too close together. As a teenager, Jennifer enrolled in New York's High School for the Performing Arts. She was not the cheerleader type. 'My parents used to scream at me because I only wore black and I had my hair cut in a modified mohawk,' she once recalled. 'My boyfriend and I looked exactly alike.' For years she carried '30 pounds more than I do now', she admitted. 'My dad used to say I had an ass you could serve tea off.' Perhaps this helped Jennifer develop her sense of comedic timing. 'I wasn't beautiful so I had to be funny,' she recalls. Although she jokes about her weight now, it wasn't until she lost over two stone that she became a star. 'It's scary,' she has said, 'how Hollywood treats you like this completely different person when you're thin.'

This is something Jen has never forgotten. Her body is one of the most admired, and fittest, in Hollywood. Jen has spoken openly about her vigorous fitness routine, which includes regular runs and incorporates budokon, a combination of martial arts, yoga and meditation. She is extremely disciplined. On the Chicago set of *The Break-*

THE NATURAL TALENT

Up, she was rumoured to have eaten only salad. During one meal, she was overheard protesting, 'I don't want any carbs!'

According to those who know her, Jennifer Aniston is a warm, highly emotional person. She was reportedly devastated by the death of her long-time therapist in December 2004, a woman who had become a surrogate mother following her estrangement from her real-life mum. Jennifer stopped speaking to her mother Nancy, an aspiring actress, after she spilled details about Jennifer's life on a talk show. The two had no contact for several years, and were only briefly reconciled in the wake of Jen's divorce.

For many years, Jen has built up a surrogate family to provide a loving network of support. Her best friend and closest confidante – *Friends* co-star Courtney Cox – has become like a sister. The two speak regularly, and Jen has just bought a home next to Courtney's. Her fondness for *Friends* co-star Matt Leblanc is well known, with Jen repeatedly referring to him as 'her brother' in interviews. She also makes sure she is never without her best friend from high school, actress Andrea Bendenwald, who travels with her everywhere, often acting as her assistant. In fact, when visiting Oprah Winfrey's home in 2005, Jennifer showed up with a gang of her closest girlfriends. When Oprah checked on her at night, she noted that, despite the fact that they each had their own bedrooms in the massive home, they were all in the same room, in the same bed, up late talking. Jen said, 'I don't even know how to explain what it is to have girlfriends like that, who are your sisters, and your mothers, and your gurus, and your mentors. They kind of just gather round. They hear the call and they're right there and I treasure it.'

In the glittering and often cruel world of show business, Jennifer Aniston surrounds herself with an entourage of people; they are not there to worship her or make her look important, but they love her very much. And, despite her divorce, she remains hopeful of finding her great romantic love. 'There's an amazing man that's wandering the streets right now who's the father of my children. In five years I would hope to be married and have a kid.'

Analyse this: Jennifer Aniston

Jennifer's relationship with her mother seems to be the biggest clue to her uncertainty about herself. Researchers have found that certain family situations can contribute towards characteristics symptomatic of the Natural Talent. More specifically, such proclivities often result when the career aspirations of the individual conflict with family expectations, and where there's a lot of conflict and expressed anger in that family.

Jennifer may also have experienced a very critical parent who put her down, making her feel confused about her own abilities – and her incredible self-discipline about her body and diet may have had its early roots in some of this negative feedback. She learned to work hard to win approval and attention in other ways, namely through acting, humour and being 'the funny one'.

It's also interesting that Jennifer was drawn to Hollywood, a notoriously critical and artificial environment – to express herself, and perhaps this mirrored her own understanding

Perfectionists – Perfectionist behaviour can lead to a host of psychological problems, but Balanced Perfectionists such as Madonna, Russell Crowe and Victoria Beckham know how to tame their perfectionism to achieve outstanding things!

Serial Romantics – it can be dangerous to be too dependent on someone's love, or too afraid of being alone. Jennifer Lopez, Julia Roberts and Brad Pitt are celebrities who've got the balance between love and independence just about right, getting the best out of their relationships.

Balanced Thrill Seekers like the highly successful Kate Moss, Angelina Jolie and Tom Cruise may feel the tension between their sensation-seeking side, and erring on the side of caution. Getting their lives in balance is something that Thrill Seekers make an enormous effort to achieve. It can work wonders, but can also be a struggle.

Nicole Kidman, Robbie Williams and Jennifer Aniston are balanced Natural Talents who play to their strengths and know how to manage those niggling doubts that often plague such a personality type.

Driven and ambitious, High Flyers are a true inspiration. The problem is that the need to achieve can become an addiction. Celebrities like Oprah, Catherine Zeta Jones and Sarah Jessica Parker manage to attain great success while understanding the importance of family and leisure – a good work-life balance!

Balanced Exhibitionists like Pamela, Jordan and Paris know just how to make their presence felt, but also understand how to tune into their emotional side, be very aware of their feelings and know how to ask for what they need.

Sharon Stone, Sharon Osbourne and Elton John (*next page*) are all larger-than-life Flamboyant Performers who know just how to be stars. They effortlessly hold centre stage yet retain the ability to empathise with the needs of others.

THE NATURAL TALENT

of herself. And it's not surprising that someone with Natural Talent tendencies might feel safe as an actor because acting involves creating a false impression, something a person with such characteristics may feel that they are doing anyway. Consequently, seeking reassurance from her other relationships and creating a network of supportive friends may have become Jennifer's healthy way to reconcile her internal conflict as she struggles to appreciate her public achievements and deal with the private hurt.

NOW ABOUT YOU

Find out: are you an extreme Natural Talent thinker?
If you answer yes to more than four of the following questions, then you could be showing symptoms associated with extremes of the Natural Talent persona:

1. Did your parents place unrealistically high expectations on you?
2. Do you often feel that many decisions affecting your life are made by other people?
3. Were you constantly compared unfavourably to other siblings?
4. Are you constantly plagued by self-doubt?
5. Was your childhood punctuated by conflict and expressed anger?
6. Are you left feeling uncomfortable if someone pays you a compliment?
7. Do you often feel that things happen to you through luck, rather than your own efforts?

8. Do you fear that you don't match up to people's expectations of you?
9. Are you worried that you could be 'found out' at any moment?

WHY DO I HAVE EXTREME NATURAL TALENT THOUGHTS?

Natural Talent characteristics can manifest themselves in different ways. You may be very successful in what you do, but have nagging doubts about yourself at the back of your mind. You may be able to see clearly the skills and talents of other people, but be completely unable to acknowledge your own abilities, or you may experience debilitating anxiety every time you are faced with a new challenge. So where do these attitudes come from?

Research has indicated that certain family circumstances create an atmosphere in which a Natural Talent style of thinking grows and takes hold. For instance:

1. You may have had parents who imposed very unrealistic and inflexible standards on you, for example labelling you as the 'the clever one', but found it hard to live up to and maintain this label as you grew older. Or...
2. You may have had aspirations that didn't fit in with your race, gender role or age. You dreamed of becoming the dynamic woman who ran her own company, or the boy who dreamed of being a hairdresser, but your aspirations were met with disapproval. Or...

THE NATURAL TALENT

3. *You may have had parents who only praised selectively. When you did well academically, your parents were delighted, but your natural ability and skill in sport went almost unnoticed.*

But, whatever the cause, the result is often the same. Those people with Natural Talent tendencies expend a lot of energy seeking reassurance from others as they struggle to balance the nagging belief that they're a fraud, despite their public success.

THE POSITIVES AND NEGATIVES

People who demonstrate Natural Talent characteristics are often high achievers and goal-orientated. They have considerable ability, drive and motivation, and the potential to achieve great success. But the problem with feeling like a fraud is that the individual is unable to accept any achievements. Consequently, Natural Talents find it hard to enjoy the moment and sometimes struggle with anxiety, depression, feelings of shame and low self-esteem.

Using the ABC model, you can see how negative automatic thoughts just below our conscious awareness affect feelings, thoughts and beliefs, even though they are often distorted and have no bearing in reality. That's exemplified by the following case history.

Josie was asked by her manager to come up with fundraising ideas for a children's charity that would bring in maximum publicity and raise awareness for the cause. Josie felt daunted by the task, but quickly put together a plan of action. She called up her contacts and set up a task force. She matched people to their strengths so that she got the best out of them. Josie raised a huge amount for the charity and won a great deal of admiration from her colleagues and manager alike. But, instead of recognising and acknowledging her natural flair and ability to lead and inspire a team, she put it all down to luck, timing and everyone else's efforts. The result? The reinforced belief that her success was down to external circumstances, and not her own ability.

What should I do if I'm like Josie?
Ask yourself the following questions:

> *What was my role in achieving success?*
> *Would my manager have asked me to carry out this task if I had very little ability to do it?*
> *Had I left things to luck and external circumstances, would I have achieved the same result?*

By standing back and being objective, you will be able to challenge both your out-of-date beliefs about yourself and your self-deprecating nature, and see how they are preventing you from recognising your talents.

Now consider the following case study. Louise had just been promoted at work. Her boss thought she was doing a fantastic job, and offered her some great perks. Louise phoned her mum to tell her all about it, but while she was talking she began to feel anxious.

THE NATURAL TALENT

Louise's mum praised her, but then worried that she wouldn't be able to cope. She told Louise to count her blessings, remarking on her good fortune in being the person who happened to get promoted. By the time Louise finished talking to her mum, she felt down and wondered whether to accept the promotion. After all, she agreed with her mum that it was luck rather than skill that had got her to where she was.

What should I do if I'm like Louise?
Take the following five steps:

1. Ditch negative messages. Start by recognising where your conflicting feelings and thoughts about yourself come from. They're not facts, they're illusions that must be countered.
2. Think back to your childhood. Were you the one in the family who was expected to fail, who wasn't going to amount to very much? And, having landed a great promotion and fantastic salary raise, would you think that this wasn't supposed to happen to you and it was all a big mistake? Does your boss's praise leave you confused and fearful that he'll find out that you are a fake? If so, work out and write down where these negative messages came from.
3. Take responsibility for your success. Write down the positive feedback from your boss regarding your promotion. Then write down all your misgivings about what he told you. By doing this,

you will clearly demonstrate to yourself the difference between objective feedback and your subjective reactions. You will also start to realise how much and how often you mistrust the opinions of other people about yourself, and how much you refuse to recognise your own abilities.
4. *Take a reality check and learn to accept your own worth. Imagine telling your boss and your work colleagues that you only got the promotion by sheer good luck, or that you tricked them into believing you are better than you actually are. Just think how daft that would sound, and imagine the looks on their faces.*
5. *Be objective – take on the role of an impartial observer and watch yourself. How would you describe yourself? Would you have given this person promotion based on their abilities? Would you say that they have a lot going for them? By doing this exercise, you will begin to recognise how others see you.*

In other words, deal positively with your negative thoughts. If you get overwhelming feelings of inadequacy, or become depressed, don't ignore it. Talk constructively about how you feel so that you can understand where your thoughts and feelings come from. If the feelings persist, they may become destructive, and result in extreme behaviour such as excess drinking and drug taking to cope with your irrational beliefs. If this happens, it's time to get professional help.

THE NATURAL TALENT

> **CELEBRITY TIP**
>
> Like Jennifer Aniston, spend time with supportive friends. Consider finding yourself a mentor, someone whom you trust and respect, a great source of encouragement who'll help you challenge your negative ideas. Turning to friends for reassurance can be an invaluable lifeline for someone with Natural Talent tendencies.

WHO NATURAL TALENTS LOVE

Safety love

If in the past you were lumbered with the wrong person, it could have been because you were attracted to someone who you thought ticked all the right boxes. Sounds familiar?

They made you feel safe because they treated you in familiar ways by putting you down, or criticising you, or ignoring your needs, or by worshipping your success. Sounds bizarre, doesn't it? (That's what happens to someone who has been psychologically criticised, or under-appreciated, or rigidly labelled, through their early years.)

Performance love

But it can happen if you find yourself with someone who is attracted to the successful and charming you. This would fit in nicely with your need to keep up a front, so there's no threat of their getting close to you and discovering that you might be a phoney. But at the same time you would have felt under pressure not to fail and let them down, which would have led to a relationship full of tension.

Critical love

Also, avoid the critical lover who puts you down, and who thinks that you exist in a supporting role. Run a mile from anyone who undermines you, or who makes you feel small. They are dumping their rubbish and their fragile ego on to you. Don't pick it up.

YOUR BIGGEST CHALLENGE

In short, if you identify with the Natural Talent, then the person for you in a relationship should have considerable emotional intelligence (or EQ). Emotionally intelligent men, as described by Daniel Goleman in *Emotional Intelligence*, are 'socially poised, outgoing, cheerful, not prone to fearfulness or worried rumination. They have a notable capacity for commitment, to people causes, for taking responsibility... they are sympathetic and caring in relationships.'

As for emotionally intelligent women, Goleman observes that they 'tend to be assertive, and express their feelings directly and to feel positive about themselves. They are outgoing, gregarious, and express their feelings appropriately (and not through outbursts, which they later regret). They rarely feel anxious or guilty, or sink into rumination.'

In addition, people with high EQ have often had plenty of life experience, and a strong sense of self.

5
The High Flyer

No one can doubt your drive and ambition, and you are an inspiration to others. Work and achievement are like food and drink to you, without which you may fear that you'll perish. Pushing yourself to the limits means that at times work means more to you than your relationships.

The psychologist David McClelland, a pioneer in the field of motivational needs theory, identified three types of motivational need. He suggested that some people possess a combination of these characteristics, but that some exhibit a strong leaning towards one particular need. And it's this bias towards a particular need, or combination of needs, that affects behaviour and thinking. The three types are…

1. *The achievement need. This person seeks challenging and achievable goals, but has a strong need for feedback about how they are doing and a sense of accomplishment.*
2. *The authority/power need. This person needs to*

THE HIGH FLYER

be influential and effective, and wants increasing personal status and prestige.

3. Affiliation motivation. This person has a need for friendly relationships driven by a need to be liked and popular.

Depending in part on childhood and past experiences, research shows that one person may be driven primarily towards making money, while another needs to gain respect, status and prestige from their peers. But the problem in being so driven is the risk of becoming addicted to the need to achieve. Research also indicates that there is a similarity between physical addiction to chemicals, such as alcohol and heroin, and psychological dependence on activities such as work, sex and sport. It's also believed that engaging in such activity may produce beta-endorphins in the brain that make you feel 'high'. This dependency can become addictive, with potentially damaging consequences.

A balanced High Flyer has the ability to achieve great things for themselves and act as an inspiration to others, and yet understand the importance and value of their family, friendships and taking time out to relax. This enables them both to be successful and to be able to enjoy the fruits of their labour.

With this in mind, let's look at three celebrities who embody the dominant features of the balanced High Flyer.

OPRAH WINFREY – THE INSPIRATIONAL HIGH FLYER

It was Oprah Winfrey's 50th birthday, and her Chicago

CELEBRITY LIFE LAUNDRY

studio was decked out with tens of thousands of roses in various shades of the superstar's favourite colours. Inside, 300 specially invited guests, along with millions of viewers, watched John Travolta make an emotional speech thanking Oprah for 'changing the lives' of millions. Tina Turner was up next, and whipped the crowd into a frenzied sing-along of her classic 'Simply the Best'. Stevie Wonder sang 'Happy Birthday' while Oprah cut into a birthday cake covered in roses and weighing more than 400 pounds. The hour-long broadcast featured taped video tributes from Nelson Mandela, Tom Cruise, Julia Roberts, Tom Hanks, Nicole Kidman, Michael Douglas and director Steven Spielberg, who congratulated Oprah on 'always getting it right'.

It was a celebration befitting a legend, which is exactly what Oprah Winfrey has become. Her power and influence on American culture is unparalleled. When President George Bush was struggling to deal with the aftermath of Hurricane Katrina, it was Oprah who set the tone of the nation's response of shock and outrage. One prominent Washington, DC, columnist wrote, 'Can someone tell President Bush to call Oprah?' *Time* magazine listed her as one of the 100 Most Influential People of the 20th century and *Newsweek* called her the Woman of the Century. She started a Book Club in 1996, and single-handedly got millions of Americans to switch off their TVs and read. She launched O, a magazine for women, in 2000 and, in a few months, it was selling millions of copies. She is said to be worth a staggering $1.3 billion.

THE HIGH FLYER

Oprah Winfrey is not your typical billionaire. Born in Mississippi to an unwed young mother, Oprah's childhood was full of poverty and pain. She was raped and sexually abused as a young girl, and suffered the trauma of becoming pregnant and losing a child at the tender age of 14. Oprah has said that her family was so poor that she made pets of cockroaches and rats. Her memories of her childhood are heart-rending. 'I grew up not feeling loved,' she once admitted. 'My greatest emotion of that time is feeling alone, but I felt special because I was such a good reader. I'd read and recite on cue, any time anybody passed by. In church, people would say, "Whoooo, this child sure can read, this child is smart." So, all my feelings of value and of being loved and appreciated came not from being nurtured by my grandmother or feeling loved by my mother, but from being able to read and perform.' While recently watching her godchild being soothed by its mother, Oprah said, 'As a child, I would have been slapped upside the head, number one. Would not even have been allowed to feel cranky. I wasn't allowed to feel what I felt. I even remember getting whippings where I would cry, then be whipped some more for crying, and then, if I would pout afterwards, get whipped again – "How dare you sit there and pout." Well, you just beat me, and I'm now supposed to express no anger or emotion or feeling about the fact that I was beat?'

Oprah's extraordinary talent emerged early on. When she was three, she would set up mock interviews with her doll and the crows on the fence outside. She was such a gifted speaker in church that her childhood nickname was 'the Preacher'. She had an early sense of her calling: 'I remember standing on the back porch and my grandmother was boiling clothes [to wash them] in a great big iron pot,' Oprah once recalled. 'I was watching her – and I remember thinking, "My life won't be like this. My life will be better."'

At 14, Winfrey went to live in Nashville, Tennessee, with her father Vernon. This marked a turning point in her early life. A strict man, Vernon ensured his young daughter got her first taste of real discipline, making her keep to a curfew and giving a report on a different book that she'd read each week. 'As strict as he was, he had some concerns about me making the best of my life, and would not accept anything less,' Oprah said.

'She has thanked me,' says Vernon, 'She said, "Daddy, if you had not been a strict disciplinarian, I would possibly be somewhere in public housing with a bunch of children."'

Instead, Oprah won a scholarship to Tennessee State University for her oratory skills, and was crowned Miss Black Tennessee. She says candidly, 'And I won beauty pageants, not because I was the most attractive but because I could always win the question-and-answer period.'

At 19, she became Nashville's first black TV news presenter. Later she was 'demoted' from news and put on a morning chat show in Baltimore. Yet the apparent setback was really the favour of a lifetime. She had found her voice: her gift was not reading the news, it was her instinctive empathy. 'I said to myself, "This is what I should be doing, it's like breathing,"' she told *Time* magazine.

THE HIGH FLYER

Oprah freely admits that she is living the life she always wanted – the one she worked and prayed for as a child. 'I have a Polaroid Swinger camera on my shelf,' she says. 'Because when I was young all I wanted was to be that girl, the Polaroid Swinger camera girl, I wanted her life, what it represented. That and that perfume, Charlie. Remember that? Char-lie [she sings the familiar jingle]. I wanted a busy, stimulating life; I wanted to go from day to night with a spritz. And even when I am dragging off the plane, I think, "This is what I wished for" and it is fantastic.'

In a recent interview with the *LA Times*, Oprah says the secret of her success is knowing what you want. 'I ask people what it is they want,' she says, 'and you would be amazed at how few of them know. They say they want to be happy. So I ask them what that happiness would look like, feel like. And they don't know. Now, I believe that the universe responds to energy, and particularly to clarity. If you focus on what you want, things clear up. If you don't, you get stuck in this muddled, fuzzy place.'

LA Times, 11 December 2005

In Oprah Winfrey's elegant and well-appointed office suite in Chicago, two figures stare solemnly out of a painting. They are African-American women, clad in long dresses, painted in charcoal on panels that run from the floor to the ceiling, 9ft high. One is seated, one is standing; around them are several wooden

> crates heaped high with pennies. They are the creation of artist Whitfield Lovell and they are called *Having*. Oprah bought the painting because of what it depicts. The portrait is of real women who owned their own sewing shop, she explains – back when 'coloured people' weren't supposed to own anything. 'I saw them in the catalogue,' she says, 'and I wanted them. But I thought they would be too big. But do you know? They fit exactly on that wall. Exactly on my wall. I felt like I was bringing them home.'

Her success did not come without struggle, though. Show bosses insisted on a complete makeover, including a hideous perm that made all her hair fall out. Afraid to say no, Oprah agreed to all the changes, only putting her foot down when asked to change her name to Suzy. At 30, she moved to Chicago to take over a failing chat show. Within a year, the programme was renamed after its new host and, by 1986, it was a national hit.

By 2005, Oprah not only owned her show but some two million shares in its distributor, King World. 'Oprah reports to nobody but God,' one of her staff once said.

'When my lawyer first came to me and said, "You can own your own show," it literally took the ceiling off my brain because I had never even thought that high before,' Oprah once revealed. 'I never even thought

THE HIGH FLYER

that was possible. Everybody needs somebody in their life to say, "Yes, you can do it!"'

Despite almost universal success, there is one area that has been a personal and very public struggle for Oprah: her weight. In 1988, after enduring a liquid diet for several months, an overweight Oprah slimmed down to a size 12 (US size 8), and then famously hauled out a wagon loaded with 67 pounds of fat, representing the amount of fat she had lost, on her show. Yet, almost as soon as she began eating again, the weight piled back on. Oprah admitted she would go home and binge eat at night, and that she once ate a bag of hot-dog buns dipped in maple syrup, just to have something to eat. She lost the weight again, ran a marathon, learned how to overcome her emotional eating, but then regained all the weight. Now, finally, at 51, she seems to have won her battle and is fitter than ever.

But this journey was not without pain. Oprah admits, 'There was a time when I had to go to this awards show and I could not fit into anything. So my stylist went and bought a very expensive suit, in a size 12, and a size 8, and they cut them and put them together to make a size 20 for me. I saw the bill for the suit and I was like, "How on earth does one suit cost that? This is ridiculous for one suit!" They were too embarrassed to tell me at first. But they did tell me. And when they did, I cried.'

In fact, Oprah's weight frequently made the headlines in newspapers and magazines. In 2005, she admitted, 'I used to read them and cry. I only just stopped reading them about three years ago. They said vile things. Everybody has a theme, and mine was that I'm fat and not married.'

Despite decades sitting comfortably on the Queen of American TV's throne, Oprah does not take her success for granted. She still works at a punishing pace. According to those who know her, Oprah works 14- to 16-hour days. Her long-time partner Stedman Graham told one reporter, 'She works very, very hard. She's up at 5.30. She's out the door at six. Then she starts her day. After work she comes home and has to get ready for the next day.'

Her daily routine also includes a 45-minute cardio workout, and 30 minutes of weight training several days a week. When she relaxes, it's the simple things that make her happy. 'I love bubble baths,' she once revealed. 'That's one big luxury I have given myself. Now that I have attained some material success, I will use an entire half bottle of bubble bath at one go. Really extravagant. And I am particular about the kind of bubbles, too. I don't want the kind that drip down off your arm. Believe me, my feet are still on the ground. I'm just wearing better shoes.'

Analyse this: Oprah Winfrey

Oprah certainly endured emotional and physical hardship in her early years. Feeling wanted and loved are the very basic ingredients of self-esteem, which Oprah by her own admission was denied. The physical and psychological trauma of being raped and then losing the baby would have caused unimaginable pain and overwhelming distress, especially to a young person. It would have had

THE HIGH FLYER

a monumental affect on her self-worth, self-esteem, self-image and confidence. Yet, out of the maelstrom of rejection, fear and heartache, she felt special because she excelled at reading.

This skill became an emotional life jacket and focus as she recognised that it set her apart, and gave her a sense of worth. Perhaps a combination of the need to achieve, her strength of character, strong desire to survive and reading skills meant Oprah was able to see a way forward. The influence of her father added the extra ingredient of discipline to her drive and motivation, laying the powerful foundation of her need to succeed.

But, despite her gift for empathising and being the wounded healer, her incredible popularity and prestige, and the knowledge that she is well loved, she appears to have emotional struggles concerning her negative relationship with food. Could her eating distress be a throwback to her early traumas? Does she use food as an emotional crutch during times of stress, emotional pain or difficulty? Oprah continues to be both brave and open in discussing these issues, using her enormous capability for self-reflection and understanding to help others to heal themselves.

SARAH JESSICA PARKER – THE CONSCIENTIOUS HIGH FLYER

As the nominees for Best Actress in a Comedy at the 2004 Emmy Awards were read out, Sarah Jessica Parker (SJ to her friends) crossed her legs and nervously fiddled with the diamond brooch at the waist of her black Chanel gown. Nominated six years in a row but never a winner, this night the prize would be hers.

She rushed on stage to accept, her diminutive figure clad in a gown of strapless lace, net and feathers, and proceeded to give the longest acceptance speech by any flushed award winner at the ceremony. She gushed thank-yous to her three co-stars, the writers, the crew and 'everybody who I had the thrill of knowing and loving and working with. And to our audience, we never took your commitment or your devotion for granted. And New York City who told the greatest story of all in the last few years… my family and my friends and my agents and my lawyer and my business manager and my publicist and passers-by who always wanted the best for me, thank you so very, very, very much.'

As over 200 million watched on television, superstar Sarah Jessica Parker revelled in what was one of the finest nights of her life. It was only as she headed towards the pressroom that the real SJ emerged for a moment and the glamorous winner quietly asked for proof of her win, grabbing the Emmy envelope as she gripped her statuette. It was so hard for her to believe. After all, it had been an epic struggle to get there.

Sarah Jessica did not always define sex for the single girl. Before her transformation into fashionista/sex columnist Carrie Bradshaw, the sharp-featured star spent years playing the leading actress's less attractive, outgoing friend. That all changed with *Sex and the City*. The hit show virtually started a cultural revolution. Here were four single women on the wrong side of 30 who should have been drowning in the sorrow of spinsterhood, but were instead living lives full of designer clothes and thrilling sex. For these women, biological clocks were unplugged: friendship and libido always won the day. And real-life women wanted to look like them. When Carrie started wearing her nameplate necklace, so did everyone else. When Carrie began wearing a huge silk flower attached to all her dresses, stores subsequently filled with them. After an episode featuring an Oscar de la Renta dress, nine of the same $3,300 dresses sold at a trunk show the next day. As Carrie, Sarah Jessica single-handedly brought back pearls, made men's tighty-whiteys look cool on girls and made any heel under 4" look like ballet slippers. Through the show, Sarah Jessica Parker had become the single woman's fantasy figure: a couture-wearing fashion icon who was spontaneously sexy, independent and forever glamorous.

But she started out life very far from the bright lights of Manhattan. Sarah Jessica was born in Nelsonville, a gritty coalmining town in Ohio. Her father, an aspiring writer, divorced his wife Barbara, with whom he had four children. Barbara, a nursery-school teacher, soon met and married another man, Paul Forste, a student and lorry driver, with whom she had four more children. With eight kids to feed, money was in short supply.

CELEBRITY LIFE LAUNDRY

Sarah admits that she sometimes finds it hard to relax. Speaking of her home life, she admits, 'I am also the orderly one. I like to go to bed with the kitchen and the toy room clean. Matthew is not really obsessed by that sort of thing. I guess he's more relaxed than I am.'

And as for her thoughts on her most famous role, that of Carrie Bradshaw? 'I've never known anyone who got to spend so much time bonding with her girlfriends as Carrie,' she says. 'I wish I had the time to do that with my girlfriends. But you know what? I don't, and you have to set your priorities. I wouldn't change them for the world.'

Sun Herald, 11 December 2005

SJP is honest about her fear of failure. 'You want to be the best you can be as an actor and the expectations that you place on yourself, and that others have for you, are big. I have this desire to please,' she confesses. Her vision of success is simple. 'What does success mean to me now? It means a full refrigerator, as many groceries as we need without worrying,' she says. 'I am busy,' she adds. 'And as long as I feel I'm giving my son everything he needs, then I guess it's better to be engaged than not to be. Sometimes I worry about being overwhelmed and overextended, but, you know, as my friend always says, "You sleep when you're dead."'

The *Independent*, 9 December 2005

THE HIGH FLYER

Sarah Jessica is still haunted by the memory of having to go to the front of her class at the age of eight to ask the teacher for a free lunch coupon. 'I remember my childhood as Dickensian. I remember being poor. There was no way to hide it. We did not have electricity sometimes. We didn't have Christmas sometimes, or we didn't have birthdays, or the bill collectors came, or the phone company would call and say, "We're shutting your phones off." Other kids always came over and played in the yard, but I don't ever recall letting our friends into the house because it was filled with old furniture. We all felt self-conscious about that for a long time.'

But Sarah Jessica's mother had big dreams for her children. Despite being on welfare, SJ was sent to ballet classes every week and began acting professionally at the age of eight. Her early career breakthrough came in 1979, at the age of 14, when she played the lead in the Broadway production of *Annie*. 'It was away from all the chaos of the house,' she says. 'It was this really structured environment. And they paid me, and I didn't have any money.'

Sarah's mother admits, 'I would like to say that I was absolutely not a stage mother. But on some level I was. But any of the kids that did not want to act didn't do it.'

Despite their financial problems, Sarah's mother Barbara attempted to model her family on another, very famous American clan: the Kennedys. Like the presidential family, Barbara was determined that her children should grow up involved in the arts and be politically active. According to SJ, 'It was about this grand idea of who we were as a family. Her role model was Rose Kennedy. She wanted to raise a family that had grand and important lives. It was weird because we were living in all this chaos, but her image was actually a great motivator.'

There was also discipline. Starting at 5.30 each morning, the lessons began. Sarah Jessica's brother Timothy recalls, 'We'd all do a 20-minute ballet class. Then Sarah would practise her violin, Pippin would practise his flute, and I would go to the piano.'

Ballet teacher David Blackburn, who taught Parker from age eight to twelve, told one reporter that Sarah Jessica was 'an extremely focused young girl'. When cast as a mouse in *The Nutcracker*, which required her to stand on her head and kick her legs when the clock struck 12, she practised devotedly at home – 'on the hour, every hour'.

Amazingly, at the age of eight, Sarah Jessica began supporting her family. The actress admits that much of the money she earned was absorbed into life at home. 'As soon as I started earning money, I contributed to the family finances.'

SJ is still very close to her siblings and parents, but her attitudes about money reflect her difficult childhood. 'The thing I want most for my children – I would like them to not be aware of money, which means I have been very aware of my financial situation,' she said. She is candid about her compulsion to keep working. 'Idle hands are the devil's workshop. My friends know how terrified I am of being broke, and they think it is hilarious and humorous,' she adds.

THE HIGH FLYER

In the summer of 1991, she began dating New York's hottest bachelor, John Kennedy Jr. One of her friends revealed, 'I remember when John asked her out on a date. She called me, screaming, "You're not going to believe who asked me out!"'

Their affair burned out quickly but ended amicably, and SJ went on to marry actor Matthew Broderick. Her initial attraction to him, as with John Kennedy Jr, seemed to be based on what he represented: the upper-middle-class, patrician, Episcopalian. When American talk-show host Larry King asked her whether her attraction to her husband was immediate, SJ replied, 'I think I liked him because he reminded me of the kind of men that my mom talked about. He was really smart and he's from this really wonderful family and he was raised in the West Village in New York and he's the funniest person I've ever known. I liked him immediately; he reminded me of memories I didn't have.'

Sarah Jessica has become the woman her mother wanted her to be. Just as her mother hoped, she has become politically active, embracing a variety of causes. Sarah Jessica has worked for voter registration, abortion rights, AIDS research, the Hollywood Women's Political Committee and UNICEF. She never swears, has given up smoking and will not do nudity. She is much more likely to be spotted with her husband at a Broadway show than in a trendy bar.

She is also defined by her work. *Sex and the City*'s producer Michael Patrick King was astounded by her compulsive work ethic. She regularly put in 14-hour days on the set during filming. He said, 'She's a leader – everyone respects her for how hard she works. Never late, never complains.'

Recently named the richest woman in New York in a magazine poll, Sarah Jessica shows no sign of slowing down. Within months of the end of *Sex and the City*, Sarah had worked on three films, launched her own fragrance and earned millions as the face of a Gap ad campaign. She is also developing scripts for HBO and still manages to make time for her three-year-old son, James Wilkie. Commenting on her rise to the top, one reporter noted, 'You don't need to work any more.' To which SJ quickly replied, 'Well, I'll always have to work, it's who I am.'

Analyse this: Sarah Jessica Parker
Sarah's childhood was a mixture of poverty, discipline and a sense of being special. Although her mother was unable to afford the best material things in life, she instilled a sense of worthiness, hard work and aspiration into her children. By setting the goalposts so high, and attempting to give her children the necessary ingredients to achieve it, she may have created an environment stressing motivation and the drive to succeed. The very act of modelling the family on the Kennedys would have inspired Sarah to set high standards and ensure she achieved them.

Since Sarah started earning and contributing to the family at a young age, she'd have felt useful and powerful. These potent ingredients reappear throughout her career, and she is known to be an extremely focused

THE HIGH FLYER

hard worker. Her attitude to money marks her out too. Perhaps her primary goal was to make money in order to feel powerful, have prestige and gain status.

However, it's possible that her identity may have become so wrapped up in making money, and thereby eliminating the possibility of ever being poor again, that she struggles to feel emotionally secure beyond her achievements. Perhaps being both driven and a great achiever enables her to gain balance and successfully manage an old insecurity – poverty.

CATHERINE ZETA JONES – THE CONSUMMATE HIGH FLYER

Catherine Zeta Jones's Cinderella fairytale became a reality when she strolled into the Grand Ballroom of New York's Plaza hotel on 12 September 2003. She was about to wed famous actor Michael Douglas, and marry into Hollywood aristocracy. The air was filled with the scent of 20,000 cream-coloured roses, while guests including Jack Nicholson and Goldie Hawn sipped some of the finest champagne in the world. Catherine, svelte and glowing after the recent birth of her baby, wore her £100,000 Christian Lacroix size-12 wedding dress and sported a diamond ring the size of a paperweight. There was also a hefty new cheque in her bank account: *OK!* magazine was paying her and Michael Douglas £1 million for the privilege of photographing the affair.

It had been a long journey from the tiny fishing village of Mumbles in Wales to the glittering lights of the Plaza.

Growing up, Catherine always had high ambitions, as did her family. The Welsh beauty has said, 'I really wanted it. I worked really hard. My parents never said, "If you're not going to college, you have to be a superstar." It was something inherently within me. There was nobody who was going to stop me.'

Catherine's star quality was obvious from an early age – at ten, she was the lead in a children's dancing troupe. Her next-door neighbour Vilma Morgan remembers her as a pretty child with dark ringlets doing dance routines in the street: 'The thing was how pretty she was. Even as a child she was always a little celebrity.'

Catherine's childhood dancing teacher, Hazel Johnson, remembers her as totally self-disciplined. 'She never wanted to go out and play, she would rather concentrate on her routines. Her talent was evident. She was brilliant at tap-dancing and got all the moves right away.'

Catherine was only 17 when she joined the chorus of the musical *42nd Street* in London. One night, when the leading lady was unable to go on, Catherine stepped into the part. Two weeks later, it was hers permanently. Her successes led to a major role in the TV series *The Darling Buds of May* – and, overnight, Catherine quickly became a household name. But she dreamed bigger.

Despite her aspirations, Catherine's first attempts at success on the big screen failed. Not easily dissuaded, she then made a disastrous attempt to launch herself as a pop star, but not one of her four singles made it past number 36 in the UK charts.

Not one to give up easily, Catherine headed straight for

THE HIGH FLYER

Hollywood, where things quickly began to change. Many people sneered that this virtual unknown, without family connections, would never make it, and yet she transformed herself into a major Hollywood player almost overnight. Steven Spielberg saw her in a television docu-drama about the sinking of the *Titanic*, and convinced Martin Campbell, director of *The Mask of Zorro*, to cast her in the film. Thus began her ascent to superstardom.

Zorro launched her film career but also nabbed her an A-list husband. Hollywood millionaire Michael Douglas saw the film and was mesmerised by the dark-haired beauty. Catherine had dated a lot of B-listers before finding her prince, including shamed television presenter John Leslie, *Soldier, Soldier* star Angus McFadyen, renowned womaniser Mick Hucknall of Simply Red and multi-millionaire Hollywood producer Jon Peters. But with Michael it was different.

> **She may hail from relatively humble beginnings in Mumbles, Wales, but these days Catherine Zeta Jones likes to travel in Hollywood style. When she was invited to attend a recent awards gala with husband Michael Douglas in New York, the Welsh actress insisted on being flown there from LA by private jet. According to the *Mail on Sunday*, Catherine likes to smoke during the fight and, as that's banned on all major airlines, private jets are her preferred method of travel.**
>
> *Mail on Sunday*, November 2005

After spotting her in *Zorro*, he arranged to sit next to her at a screening at the Deauville Film Festival. His opening line was, 'I'd like to be the father of your children.' Speaking about Catherine's life before him, Michael said dismissively, 'She'd been with her fair share of idiots.' But that was now all in the past.

In describing Catherine, the two words that pop up most often are ambition and determination. 'Catherine is straightforward, gutsy, with no ego, and no bullshit,' says Liam Neeson, who co-starred with her in *The Haunting*. 'She worked hard and created her own luck, which is something I share with her. She was always the first on the set, and she never ran out of energy, even though, Christ, we were running so much on that movie, and she was in high-heeled boots. I used to call her the Welsh Gazelle.'

Catherine admits, 'I'm openly ambitious. I'm terrible. At Scrabble or Trivial Pursuit, I just have to win. If I don't, I'm a nightmare. It's always been a thing for me, from swimming to judo, to dancing or singing. People make the analogy between determination and ruthlessness – this bitch quality, that I'll go anywhere and do anything to get what I want.' But Catherine says her ambition is of a friendlier sort. 'I'm not like that. I'm ambitious, but I'm openly ambitious. What I bring to the table is completely different from what somebody else will bring. So there's room for everybody.' And she adds, 'I'm strong because I've had to be.'

Catherine often refers to her work ethic. 'I got here on my own bloody hard work and perseverance,' she insists. 'You've got to work hard, and you've got to be able to

THE HIGH FLYER

string a sentence together. I think I can do both. I don't want to sound arrogant,' she adds, 'but I'm aware that I'm an attractive woman and that carries with it a certain responsibility. I do have ambition, but I'm not ruthless. I don't want to look back and know I didn't give it my best shot.'

Catherine's life today resembles that of royalty. Now worth £170 million, she is Wales's wealthiest woman. With her husband, Michael Douglas, she enjoys luxurious residences in Los Angeles, New York, Aspen, Bermuda, Swansea and Majorca. As Catherine says, 'My life now is like going through the closet into Narnia. I opened the door and walked into this magical place.'

A close friend told one newspaper, 'Catherine is living out every single one of her childhood fantasies. Her life is just incredible. She lives like a princess and mixes with the most famous people in the world.'

Catherine most often flies by private jet and receives frequent Cartier gifts, her favourite jeweller, from her devoted husband. ('Call me old-fashioned, but nothing says "I love you" like a big old rock.') It's a royal lifestyle and, as Michael Douglas says, 'What Catherine wants, Catherine gets.'

Her grand attitude does not sit well with everyone but, in a town driven by image and status, Catherine has most certainly become the Queen.

Analyse this: Catherine Zeta Jones

Catherine has experienced a meteoric rise from humble beginnings to Hollywood royalty. But how did she do it?

CELEBRITY LIFE LAUNDRY

She came from a family with great aspirations for her. It seems that from a very early age she had a real sense of her worth and, perhaps, an idea of what she could achieve. A family environment where a child is consistently praised for certain qualities including hard work, achievement and success, as well as being made to feel special, may well develop a very powerful sense of value. Certainly, a combination of natural good looks, an encouraging environment and her own persistence enabled her to aim high.

Catherine had the drive and motivation to be ambitious, gaining prestige, status, and power along the way. Like all high achievers, her focus and drive meant that setbacks never became major impediments. And having worked so hard to get to the top, it's no surprise that she fiercely guards her achievements and sense of accomplishment. She has turned her own fantasy into reality.

NOW ABOUT YOU

Find out: are you an extreme High Flyer?
If you answer yes to more than four of the following, you could be an extreme High Flyer:

1. Do you make long-term goals?
2. Does hard work and persistence make you come alive?
3. Do you often ignore health worries if you have a deadline to meet?

THE HIGH FLYER

4. Did you come from a home where achievement and hard work were highly prized?
5. Do you often forget birthdays and anniversaries because you are so absorbed in work?
6. Do you sometimes feel anxious if you are not working on your next project?
7. Is socialising less important to you than work?
8. Do you feel that your success doesn't satisfy you for long?

WHY AM I AN EXTREME HIGH FLYER?

A combination of factors shape a High Flyer. Past experiences, environment and family all play their part.

Family childhood certainly has an influence. In *Human Motivation*, Bernard Weiner argues that a high-achieving male tends to have rejecting parents who expected him to become independent early, gave him high demands and rewarded his success and/or punished unsatisfactory behaviour. According to Grace Baruch in her article 'Girls who Perceive themselves as Competent', female high achievers tend to have non-traditional, permissive parents who rewarded their achievements. They come from families in which the mother plays a crucial role.

Growing up in an environment where achievement and being independent early on is highly prized can also have long-lasting repercussions, because you then strive to reinforce this behaviour by seeking out people who value it.

CELEBRITY LIFE LAUNDRY

THE POSITIVE AND NEGATIVES

Being a High Flyer can be an amazing experience. Psychologist David McClelland firmly believes that achievement-motivated people are generally the ones who make things happen and get results.

However, being an extreme High Flyer can cause you problems. Your drive and ambition may make you too self-absorbed. And being so single-minded may affect your close relationships. You may even find that your health suffers as you strive so hard to succeed.

Read the following case history and see what happens when work and achievements become more valuable than family and friends.

Lyn had a big presentation at work coming up, one that could lead to a very lucrative promotion. She spent months working on it, in the evenings and at weekends, but her partner was starting to complain and feel neglected. The kids were playing up because she was always researching on the internet, and her friends became frustrated because she rejected all their invitations.

But Lyn couldn't understand what everyone was complaining about. She strongly believed that getting promoted was the most important thing in her life, and would lead to an even bigger promotion the following year. She felt frustrated, angry and tense because those close to her were demanding all her time, and she ended up rowing with her partner, storming out and feeling that no one appreciated what she was trying to do.

THE HIGH FLYER

What should I do if I'm like Lyn?

Use your skills of assessment. How true is it that, if you take one hour out of your day to spend with the family, it will cost you the promotion?

Ask yourself how many times you have promised your kids that you'll take them out, only to cancel or forget.

Ask yourself what do you stand to lose if you carry on like this. Your health? Marriage? Family?

By doing this, you will start to reassess your behaviour. Then consider Katie's position, in the following case history, and see if it throws any light on your own.

Katie came from a single-parent family. Her parents divorced when she was 11, and she lived with her mum and her two younger sisters. Before Katie's father left, her mum had been at home full time raising the family, but since the divorce she had to go out to work to earn extra money. She took on two part-time jobs and worked long hours. She never complained, and encouraged her children to work hard. Katie washed cars in her street for pocket money, did a paper round and took responsibility at home for her sisters. Her mum was very proud of her efforts, and Katie felt good that she was helping the family, but also felt that she had to hide negative feelings and worries from her mum because she didn't want to let her down.

Katie was determined to do very well at school, and was driven to achieve. She worked hard, and her efforts were rewarded, later earning her a first-class degree. She went on to business school, and became a High Flyer in the city. Soon she was earning big money, and achieving great things. Although she hardly had any time for fun or relationships, this didn't seem to bother her. True, she sometimes suffered from headaches and frequently felt tired, but she ignored these symptoms and carried on working long hours.

One day, while at work, she collapsed from exhaustion and was rushed to hospital. She was run down and burned out. But still Katie couldn't figure out why this had happened.

What should I do if I'm like Katie?

> 1. *Break the chain. You may be unaware of what drives you so hard, so think back to your early childhood. What were the family's expectations (whether articulated or not) of you? Not that looking back means casting blame or feeling hard done by – it's a tool that'll enable you to see what messages influenced you. Also ask yourself, what was it that you achieved and prized above everything else? How were negative feelings dealt with? And were the expectations set for you by your parents very high? By answering these questions honestly, you'll notice patterns of belief and behaviour that you now re-enact as an adult.*
> 2. *Take a break. Your self-discipline and driven*

THE HIGH FLYER

nature may be tremendous attributes, but working ridiculous hours will take its toll, affecting your health, diet and friendships. In fact, research shows that these three areas are vital ingredients for stress and anxiety reduction. If you carry on with bad habits, eventually your body will rebel and stop.

3. *If you find that you are constantly run down and suffering ill health, then you are in danger of approaching exhaustion and burnout. Listen to your body, and act immediately. Don't eat on the run, and don't stay strapped to your computer for hours. Take walks, enjoy meals and look after yourself.*

4. *Pay attention to others. Being a High Flyer means that you have managed to achieve many of your aims. The problem is that you may have been so single-minded in achieving your goals that you may have neglected your friendships. If that's the case, you may end up with no one to turn to during difficult times, and may be likely to suffer bouts of loneliness. Learning to recognise that you are not the sum total of what you achieve, and that other people in your life can add value through friendship, is a vital step forward.*

> **CELEBRITY TIP**
>
> You may be hell-bent on providing the best for your family, possessing a strongly held belief that prestige and status is what it's all about, but stop and examine what is really going on. Ask yourself, 'When will I know that I am satisfied?' The answer may well be 'never'. This is your opportunity to explore other areas. Charity work? Helping underprivileged children? You might well find it more rewarding than anything else you've ever done.

HIGH FLYERS IN LOVE

Focused

In the past, you may have approached relationships with the same dogged determination that you apply to your professional life. Your criteria may have been very specific and, with your future plans in place, you may have looked for a person who matched you financially, echoed your aspirations or had also achieved a lot of success. There is nothing wrong with that. But potential problems may have occurred if your loved one stopped doing well, demanded more of your time than you were prepared to give, or couldn't fit into your busy schedule.

THE HIGH FLYER

Lonely

Your biggest challenge is therefore to let someone in to your life. Being motivated by achievement and success involves tremendous energy but, strangely, the experience can leave you empty. You may be so focused on going the extra mile that you become self-absorbed, squeezing out closeness and intimacy. You may become so addicted to your own achievement that you leave loved ones feeling redundant.

THE HEALTHY RELATIONSHIP FOR YOU

Being a High Flyer, you may have at times alienated those closest to you in your determined pursuit of greatness and recognition. You may use work as a way to avoid looking at feelings and emotions, and use the protective defence of burying yourself in work as a wonderful method of avoiding emotional closeness.

Understanding that this might have happened in the past is the greatest step towards making a space in your life for love and intimacy. The right person for you will bring spontaneity and warmth. They will encourage you to view life not as a race that you have to win, but as one packed with rewarding experiences. They won't see you as the sum total of your achievements, but will value you for who you are, and will love your vulnerability. A person like this is worth their weight in gold.

6
The Exhibitionist

Operating like an Exhibitionist means that people simply can't ignore you. You know how to grab attention, or how to make an entrance, whether it's being the loudest, brashest person, or the one wearing the least amount of clothes. You are dramatic and love attention. But the Exhibitionist has a flip side, often initially difficult to detect. You may be someone who acts like a doormat or puts up with being treated badly by your partner. You may be the one who rescues others from their problems, yet deep down craves love and attention.

Research by Dr Janet Kizziar, who specialises in working with troubled families, shows that those who come from unsettled environments and who regularly experienced emotional upsets may have developed a certain set of survival characteristics to deal with it.

This type of person may cope by creating a tough outer layer or mask in order to manage their true feelings. They may be the rescuer, the comedian or the sexy show-off, but they also make sure that no one knows how they really feel deep down.

THE EXHIBITIONIST

According to research, a number of key emotional areas can be affected if the individual becomes an extreme of this personality type. An out-of-balance individual may:

1. *Have difficulty in forming and maintaining close and intimate relationships.*
2. *Experience a higher-than-normal incidence of marrying a person from another troubled family*
3. *Constantly need and seek out approval from others.*
4. *Act belligerently and aggressively to keep others at a distance.*
5. *Have exaggerated feelings of shame, worthlessness and low self-esteem.*

A balanced person with Exhibitionist tendencies will know just how to make their presence felt, but will also understand how to tune into their emotional side, be very aware of their feelings and know how to ask for what they need.

With that in mind, let's look at three celebrities who reflect the qualities of the balanced Exhibitionist.

PAMELA ANDERSON – THE SEXY EXHIBITIONIST

'I wanted to retire from all that, but I guess my breasts still have a career and I'm just tagging along with them. I know *Baywatch* was mindless, but it was a great show. You could turn it on halfway through in any language and still be entertained. But the fact is, I'm kind of proud of myself. I have the PETA projects, I'm a working soccer mom to my two boys and I try to do what I can in the community. I think I've been able to keep a certain grace about me even during times of disgrace and craziness which have swallowed me up in the past.' Pamela Anderson

Pamela Anderson's wedding to musician Kid Rock was far from your average walk down the aisle. The bride wore a Heatherette mini-dress, which she quickly tore off to reveal a skimpy white string bikini, all the while her long-haired groom drank beer. It was an anything-goes, music-blaring, champagne-swilling throwdown.

'The best thing about today was the sheer fun of it all,' said guest David Furnish, 'It was a real rock and roll wedding.' The fact that the marriage wasn't legal – French law requires three months' residency – didn't dampen anyone's spirits, least of all the ecstatic bride. As she put it on a posting on her website, 'It was the best, most romantic wedding of all time.' And it was a long time coming. The on-and-off romance between Pam and the Detroit rocker was a rollercoaster ride dating back to 2001. After a broken engagement in 2002, the pair ran into each other three years later on a mutual friend's yacht in Saint-Tropez. 'It was like we'd never been apart,' Kid told reporters. And following a whirlwind courtship, the second time around proved to be even sweeter for the couple. Their wedding celebrations ended with a dance-off among the 150-odd guests, including model Cindy Crawford and designer Tommy Hilfiger, while Pam and

THE EXHIBITIONIST

her new groom duetted on a karaoke version of the Rolling Stones' 'Sympathy for the Devil'.

It was the summer of 1989 when the 22-year-old Pamela Anderson put on a tight T-shirt and curled her hair for the British Columbia Lions football game in Vancouver. She had no idea that this day was going to change her life forever. The pretty blonde was enjoying the match with some girlfriends when a camera linked to the big screens at the stadium picked her out of the crowd. Every time the camera alighted on the busty bombshell, the crowd cheered. Thanks to her choice of T-shirt – displaying the Labatt's beer logo – the company immediately offered her a modelling contract and she became their 'Blue Zone Girl'.

It was the start of something big for the fitness instructor. She had a killer body, a smouldering smile and she made the most of showing herself off. Sexy adverts for the beer company went down well with the scouts from *Playboy* magazine, who offered her a centrefold. Pamela jumped at their offer to pose naked, but not before getting her first set of breast implants. She was off to Hollywood.

Her first appearance in the October 1989 issue of *Playboy* became a bestseller and she went on to feature on the cover a record 11 times. Her next big break followed in the form of a tight red swimsuit. One billion people in more than 140 countries tuned in to watch Pamela running in slow motion through the Californian surf on the hit TV show *Baywatch*. She had used her assets to become the sexiest, most lusted-after woman in the world.

CELEBRITY LIFE LAUNDRY

Today, there are more than 145,000 websites devoted to Pamela Anderson's breasts. In fact, she often speaks about them in interviews. 'My breasts – it's a love–hate thing, but we're very close,' she says. Following her divorce from ex-hubby rocker Tommy Lee, Pamela had her implants removed. 'I got divorced so I did what every girl does. I cut my hair and took out my boobs... It was like, "I'll show him."' At the time Pam said of her new downsized look, 'This is the best thing I ever could have done. I feel really good. I feel much sexier. I'm running around naked all the time now. It was already hard for me to keep my clothes on, but now – forget it.'

But the smaller version of Pam didn't last for long; she missed her bigger breasts or perhaps the attention they brought. The actress soon had them put back in, bigger than ever.

Pamela Anderson's love life has been volatile. She married Mötley Crüe drummer Tommy Lee after a four-day romance. The ceremony was performed on a beach in Cancun, Mexico, and in lieu of a wedding dress she wore a tiny white bikini. The honeymoon was action-packed – and videoed. The couple claimed that the video in question was later stolen from the safe of their Malibu home and posted on the internet. The explicit video involved a wild array of sexual gymnastics. Nowadays celebrity sex videos on the internet seem commonplace, but, in the early 1990s, Pamela was the first big star caught on camera *in flagrante delicto*. The X-rated video made millions, and, despite vehement denials from the couple, some cynics alleged the tape was released on purpose.

THE EXHIBITIONIST

In interviews, the couple spoke openly about their sex life. Anderson loved to tell stories of how she would go naked across the living room on an overhead swing while Tommy played the grand piano below her.

However, the romance turned sour and there were reports of Lee's addiction to alcohol and violent behaviour. Eventually, his violence towards his wife earned him a seven-month jail sentence. During his absence, Pammy had a 'Tommy' tattoo on her finger changed to read 'Mommy'.

Despite her previous experience with rock stars, she then began dating wildman Kid Rock. The two of them seemed to find real passion and a mutual love for sex outside the bedroom. Just before they split, Pamela and Kid were photographed fondling each other outrageously in front of startled witnesses at a party before the Kentucky Derby.

> **Pamela Anderson may be the world's most desired mum, as she has now appeared on the cover of men's magazine *Playboy* a record-breaking 11 times. After posing in April 2004, 15 years after she first graced the mag's cover, Pamela said, 'I love that I can still do *Playboy*, especially as some people don't approve of it. After all these years, people are still hung up about it. Look at the reaction to Janet Jackson's nipple. I understand that you aren't expecting to see a breast while you're watching the Superbowl. But I don't understand the outrage. Over a nipple? Come on.**

CELEBRITY LIFE LAUNDRY

> When people pretend sexuality isn't part of our lives, ugly stuff comes out.'
>
> Pamela Anderson ditched playboy former motor-racing driver Eddie Irvine because he wasn't wild enough. The pair enjoyed a brief fling in the spring of 2006, but former *Baywatch* babe Pammy insists the Irishman is too much of a gentleman. She says, 'I met him through friends and he's a good friend of mine. Eddie was just too sweet for me.'
> *Contact News*, 26 June 2006

This blonde superstar started out life far away from the bright lights and glitz of Hollywood. Pamela Anderson was born in a small town in British Columbia on 1 July 1967. While she was growing up, her mother was a waitress in a pancake house and her father was a logger with a drink problem (although he has since reformed and is now very close to his daughter). This rather volatile and troubled childhood forged a strong relationship between Anderson and her mother. 'We've always been real close and talked about everything, which has been real helpful,' she says. Pam had unconventional aspirations, even as a child: 'I wanted to be a stripper when I was a little girl,' she once admitted. 'Most of my friends wanted to be nurses or lawyers, but I wanted to take my clothes off.' She was a character even then. 'I was always in trouble; I was a drama queen right from a very young age.' She's still very devoted to

THE EXHIBITIONIST

her brother and has said that he and her mother are the two steadying influences in her life.

Those who know her say she is misunderstood and that, contrary to her vixen image, she is bright, funny and caring. When she's off-camera, she prefers the natural, no make-up look, walks around in sweat pants and is often found cheering from the sidelines at one of her two young sons' baseball games. Pam says, 'The public image is about 5 per cent of who I really am. And the other 95 per cent, the fact that I'm a hardworking actress, an executive producer and, most important of all, the mother of two small boys, well, that all gets lost. Sometimes I do pick up the papers and read about myself and wonder, "Who the hell are they talking about?"'

Despite her predilection for micro-minis and stiletto heels, in real life, Pam is a lot less glam. 'I'm a tomboy, the least girly girl you could think of,' she claims. 'I didn't wear a stick of make-up until I came to LA. I never thought of myself as a pretty woman. I still don't. And I don't like any pictures of myself. I like doing them and I like taking them. I take amazing pictures of my kids. But I don't have photos of myself around my house. I'm somewhat of an exhibitionist but I don't like seeing the finished product. My mother and my brother have scrapbooks of my pictures but not me. [Photographer] David LaChapelle told me, "You're the only person I've every photographed that doesn't want to see the pictures. I have to beg you to look at them."'

In fact, she was so self-conscious about how she might seem on-camera that ex-hubby Tommy Lee was never allowed to watch an episode of *Baywatch*. 'I wouldn't let anybody watch anything,' she admits. And, despite her history of public disrobing, Pam says her image is really not her. '*Playboy* is really a different side of me that I didn't know was there,' she says. 'There's the person who lives inside my head, and the person I really am.'

Pamela Anderson is nothing if not shrewd about her career. She has starred in three major TV series, including her latest – the appropriately named *Stacked*. She promotes her own range of lingerie, swimwear, sunglasses, jewellery, and even clothing and accessories for dogs. She represents MAC cosmetics and is a spokesperson for People for the Ethical Treatment of Animals (PETA). She has also written two novels, which she claims are based only very loosely on her life. The dust jacket of one is a prime taster for what lies between the covers: a naked upper-body shot of Pam with a large star covering her breasts.

It will be interesting to see how Pamela defines herself as she approaches 40. After all, sex symbols don't tend to have a very long shelf life. Perhaps anticipating this, she recently announced that she is shifting her career away from her most famous assets. 'I'm 38 and I don't need to get them out any more,' she said at an event in Hollywood. 'My mom told me I've got beautiful eyes and a beautiful smile, that's what a man wants to see…'

Analyse this: Pamela Anderson

Pamela has the reputation for being the classic Exhibitionist. However, instead of wondering who she is,

THE EXHIBITIONIST

and what makes her tick, it seems that Pamela has reduced herself simply to a timeless image – the blonde bombshell. Yet there is a duality about her persona; though it's enticing, it is also depersonalised and one is left wondering who she is.

She has tapped into man's primal desire through her breasts, and for a long time her identity has been wrapped up in her looks – specifically, her chest – so much so that, when she's had a breast reduction, she has found herself feeling strangely invisible. Perhaps without her ample breasts, the real Pamela feels uncertain and insecure. With the infamous video tape, she has even turned the intimate and private into a public performance – albeit unintentionally. This sense of danger and daring has left her at the hands of abusive experiences, perhaps mirroring her volatile childhood. That childhood involved emotional disruptions, unpredictability and inconsistency. Having a parent with a drink problem certainly created tensions at home, and perhaps this forced the young Pamela to grow up faster and keep the family problems a secret. In this kind of environment, the child's own needs and wants may well have taken second place. Pamela may have learned to play down her own feelings from an early age.

Now, in adulthood, Pamela at times seems alienated from the persona she has created and become stuck with. Has she perhaps discovered that being the sum total of her breasts has meant she's misunderstood? When Pamela declares that her public image is only five per cent of who she really is, that's a big clue that she feels trapped by her own creation and is engaging in what we call 'double messaging'. She may feel that only a minor part of her is what we see, but she has certainly invested a great deal of energy in promoting this armour. Perhaps having such an unpredictable childhood has left its mark. Her assets have given the audience a focus, and that has certainly diverted attention away from the other 95 per cent of Pamela Anderson.

JORDAN – THE BLATANT EXHIBITIONIST

The biggest wedding of 2005 was not just a ceremony; it was a lavish media circus – more a publicity extravaganza than publicity stunt. The bride's wedding dress was covered in thousands of pink Swarovski crystals, and she rode to the ceremony in a glass carriage pulled by six miniature white ponies. Dozens of white doves were released into the air as she arrived. Her train was so long it crossed the entrance into the austere Highclere Castle minutes after she did. The romantic yet strangely ironic harmonies of the choir joined on Whitney Houston's 'I Have Nothing', which blended softly with the sound of helicopters full of photographers hovering above. However, on the ground, a team from *OK!* magazine voraciously snapped every second of Jordan's wedding to Peter Andre, as part of an elaborate deal worth an estimated £2 million.

Jordan is a celebrity revelation. Her command of the glossy pages in Britain is unrivalled, but she has not starred in a film, released a single or selflessly served a

THE EXHIBITIONIST

leading charity. She is a new breed of celebrity who, by her tireless exhibitionism and self-promotion, has used the press to become a brand-new feature.

She began as a Page 3 girl in the *Sun*, and quickly became an 'It Girl' for the masses. She arrived scantily clad at parties all over London, and frequently lifted up her skirt or top to flash for the photographers. And, in addition to the dozens of men's magazine covers featuring her overly voluptuous figure, there was the essential item of any self-respecting Exhibitionist's list of achievements: the internet sex video. Jordan's fans all over the world downloaded footage of her *in flagrante delicto* while visibly pregnant.

Jordan's love life has helped elevate her status, and increase the inches devoted to her in gossip columns. After her first serious boyfriend, failed pop star Dane Bowers, she engaged in a string of high-profile romances. She became pregnant by footballer Dwight Yorke, and had an affair with young singer Gareth Gates.

The reality-TV show that turned Jordan into a household name was *I'm A Celebrity… Get Me Out Of Here!*. Through that one programme, the glamour model broke into the mainstream media and emerged as a surprisingly sympathetic character. She was down-to-earth, amiable and warmly supportive of the other contestants. She also managed to pick herself up a husband, fellow contestant and pop star Peter Andre. And, if there were any doubts about Jordan's business skills, they were dispelled after it emerged she had negotiated a £100,000 fee for her appearance on the programme – more than four times the fee that any other contestant received.

CELEBRITY LIFE LAUNDRY

After *I'm A Celebrity...*, Jordan dumped her long-time manager to sign up with Can Associates, a PR firm that already had Andre on its books. And thus was born another reality-TV show – *When Jordan Met Peter* – this time dedicated entirely to the intimate details of their newfound love.

Not content with baring her body, Jordan has also bared her soul with her autobiography *Being Jordan*. The book hit the bestseller lists, with the public snapping up close to half a million copies. In it, she speaks openly of her desire for celebrity and speaks candidly about her sex life, at some points in cringe-making detail. She is a celebrity who seems determined to hide nothing from her fans.

> **Jordan has created an empire based on her infamous physique. She is set to unveil a brand-new range of lingerie and the sexy star made a small fortune from her range of jewellery at Argos, based on her boobs. According to store figures, the tasteful pieces – which include such delights as earrings shaped like thongs and bras and T-shirts with 'Slapper', 'Slag' or 'Golddigger' emblazoned across the chest – fairly flew off the shelves.**

Jordan was born Kate Infield in Brighton in 1978, but her childhood didn't last for long. Her parents separated when she was just four, after which she was brought up by her mother. (When her mum eventually remarried, Kate Infield became Katie Price.) In total, the family

THE EXHIBITIONIST

(including her brother and sister) moved house 13 times over the following few years. By the age of 13, Katie had begun doing photo shoots, and by 15 she was dating an ex-convict who was violent towards her.

Katie seemed to figure out at an early age that her precocious good looks and enhanced figure was a quick ticket to money and success. She is said to have gone to her local cosmetic surgery clinic at 16 to ask for a breast enlargement, only to be told she was too young. Eventually, she had her first operation at the age of 18, and since then has had at least two more, taking her to a 32FF bra size.

Katie first became known as Jordan after appearing on Page 3 of the *Sun*. The name seemed to suit her, allowing Katie to adopt a new racier persona. In interviews, Jordan has talked about having two personalities, the nice girl Katie Price and her outrageous alter ego Jordan. According to Jordan, Katie is a sweet girl who grew up in Brighton, while Jordan is an extrovert Exhibitionist who seeks to be lusted after and adored by all. As one friend told the papers, 'It's as if Jordan gives her permission to do the things Katie daren't do.'

Jordan is a tabloid-culture heroine; her success rides on the size of her breasts and her willingness to show them off. While she is currently striving to develop a singing and acting career, her intrinsic value is in the image she has created herself: the walking, talking Barbie doll, shrewdly capitalising on the fantasies of millions of men. In an industry that seeks only to titillate and entertain, she is a creator and conqueror.

CELEBRITY LIFE LAUNDRY

Analyse this: Jordan

Exposure seems to be Jordan's middle name. Describing herself as an Exhibitionist, and going out of her way to reveal almost every inch of her body, appears to be her modus operandi. On the one hand, she has made a huge financial success out of being like this. She has created the perfect image for the male market, ensuring sure-fire success. However, there are two distinct sides to her.

The biggest insight into Jordan as a person came when she famously participated in *I'm A Celebrity....* She appeared to work very hard to lose Jordan, the sex-bomb image she'd worked so hard to create, and instead presented a quieter Katie Price, inviting her fellow participants and the viewers to observe her new identity. Fascinatingly, she did it in the biggest public arena that she could find. However, she also engaged in psychological double messaging by still needing Jordan as a protective power shield.

She came out of the jungle more famous, and with a public romance and marriage under her belt. It seems that, no matter what she's doing, she invites the public to have a look, whether she's getting married, having a baby or coping with a sick child. She appears to invite the public in to her life, letting them assume the role of surrogate parents. What does she gain from this relationship with the public? Mainly attention, though she does maintain control by keeping an emotional distance.

From a relatively early age, it seems that her sexuality was a means of survival. Her childhood certainly seemed emotionally and psychologically disrupted, and with all

THE EXHIBITIONIST

this instability the young Katie would have been seeking a way to cope. There seems to have been no firm parental voice to offer consistent boundaries, and teach her how to curb her behaviour. Using her body and looks as a way out of difficulties, she grew up fast, and may have used her sexy image as a way of handling a wide range of needs, wants, anger and/or disappointments.

There seems to be a childlike innocence about her, and she reveals much about herself in a frank and open way that endears you to her, yet she also shows a fiercely shrewd business side that has made her a very rich woman. But what does Katie really want? To be loved for who she is without needing to hide behind Jordan? Perhaps that is her biggest emotional challenge.

PARIS HILTON – THE ALLURING EXHIBITIONIST

Asked about the Paris Hilton sex video, Pamela Anderson had one observation: 'She should have kept her shoes on.'

Paris Hilton is a blonde and beautiful heiress to a fortune of some $30 million. She is also one of America's most famous It Girls. Her reputation for a love of the high life and coast-to-coast partying began when she was still a teenager and she quickly became ripe fodder for American gossip columns.

As the great-granddaughter of Conrad Hilton, founder of the Hilton hotel chain and one-time husband of Zsa Zsa Gabor, Paris was born into one of America's most famous families. She could have easily morphed into one of New York's society dames, lunching in pearls and heels, but her big break came in the form of an amateur sex video. The filmed bedroom escapade of the heiress – then 19 – and ex-boyfriend Rick Solomon was the subject of countless headlines around the world.

In the video, Paris is seen cavorting naked in front of the camera, vamping it up and showing off her breasts in the bathroom, where she says the lighting is better. When the tape became public, Paris sued to stop it, saying, 'I feel embarrassed and humiliated, especially because my parents and the people who love me have been hurt. I was in an intimate relationship and never, ever thought these things would become public.'

When it seemed clear that the tape was going to be released with or without her consent, Paris reached a deal. She was given $400,000 and a percentage of the profits.

After the sex tape's release, Paris found her status elevated from semi-glamorous, B-list party guest smiling sexily for the paparazzi to that of an international star. The tape became a spectacular episode of self-promotion. By the time Paris's new reality show *The Simple Life* hit TV screens, just one week after the video hit the internet, everyone knew who Paris Hilton was. The first episode achieved ratings far beyond the dreams of network bosses, and outdid an address to the nation by President Bush that same night.

Paris quickly began to trade on her sexed-up image. She starred in the notoriously racy and controversial commercial for Carl's Jr, a California hamburger chain, which featured her dressed in a tiny leather bathing suit, writhing around with a bucket of soapy water and a garden hose while washing a Bentley. She also posed for an 11-page spread in *Vanity Fair* magazine, pictured sprawled on a Malibu beach, in a sheer dress pulled down to reveal one breast and up to show off her G-string knickers, while a group of California surfers stood by admiringly. As her notoriety increased, people found themselves asking, 'What is it exactly that she does, again?'

No one can deny that Paris has worked hard at becoming famous for being famous. And though she may have entered the celebrity arena through sex, she has certainly branched out since. *The Simple Life* is in its fifth season, and Paris is now a producer. She has had roles in several films and can earn $200,000 just for turning up at a party for 20 minutes. ('If it's in Japan I get more,' she once revealed.) She has launched two Paris Hilton perfumes, and is now working on a cologne for men. There is a Club Paris in Orlando, Florida, in Las Vegas and Miami. Her jewellery range for Amazon.com is in the internet store's top 20 products for sales. Her book, *Confessions of an Heiress*, hit the *New York Times* bestseller list in 2004. Her first album has received generally decent reviews and she is now planning a chain of boutique hotels. All this, while exhausting millions of flash bulbs walking along miles of red carpets, normally in tiny bits of fabric and impossibly high stiletto heels.

Despite her real-life sexual escapades, now immortalised on tape, Paris has always claimed that her love life is more mundane than people believe. She has been linked to a variety of men, including Leonardo DiCaprio, model Jason Shaw, former fiancé Greek shipping heir Paris Latsis, and Greek millionaire Stavros Niarchos. However, Paris insists she has a low sex drive and frequently says no to steamy sessions with her men: 'I'm sexual in pictures and the way I dress and my whole image, but at home I'm really not like that. All of my ex-boyfriends would be like, "What's the matter with you? You're so not sexual."'

> Nicole Richie, former best friend to Paris Hilton, features a villain in her novel *The Truth About Diamonds* that sounds suspiciously like her former friend Paris. The character is 'a model, actress and an all-around professional fake-rich girl' named Simone Westlake. Richie claimed that the character is a composite of several people. However, Simone's description seems a spot-on characterisation of Paris. Simone is a 'back-stabbing blonde model/actress with fake breasts who takes her chihuahua everywhere, makes sex videos and accidentally "loses" her mobile phone, which is full of celebrity phone numbers'.

Paris grew up on the West Coast, and in 1996 moved to New York, where her father opened a branch of his real-estate office. Paris attended several private schools on both coasts, including a school for troubled kids in Utah. At the age of 17 she left school and enrolled at a fashion college in LA, but then left to take a 'year off'. That was the end of school for her – and the beginning of the party girl Paris.

THE EXHIBITIONIST

She spent more than five years living on the 30th floor of the Waldorf-Astoria hotel, part of the Hilton hotel empire. Despite being able to call one of the world's most luxurious places home, Paris was not always happy there: 'When you can just order all the time, it's not fun any more.' In France, where she's less well known, Paris has been known to announce to people, 'I am American royalty.' Of course, she has been bred to be a star. In fact, that's her family's nickname for her – as her mum Kathy says, 'Star just does what she wants.'

Paris is a girl who truly loves her celebrity. Born with a financial freedom that most of us will never know, Paris does not need to work. And yet she was driven to make her name famous across the world. In truth, she has become more than a name – she is her own brand. She flaunts her sexuality without shame, although there are signs that there are moments of self-realisation. 'We're nice girls,' Paris recently said to a room full of reporters, referring to herself and her younger sister, Nicky. She paused, looked around the room and then added, 'It's not my fault.'

Analyse this: Paris Hilton

Paris has it all, materially speaking: money, looks, everything. So why would she go out of her way to gain attention by using her sexuality in a provocative manner, and choose to make a name for herself in such an extrovert way?

Perhaps the biggest clue to Paris is the fact that she has everything at her fingertips, without having to work for it, and yet at the same time has grown up rapidly with seemingly few boundaries to regulate her developing sexuality. This can leave a gap. She may wonder who she is underneath.

Her good looks mean she can use her sexuality as her main identity. People give her the attention she craves, and she shrewdly capitalises on it. This has clearly become a quick, easy way to be noticed as she has possibly attempted to create a different identity and find her own way. The rumour that she had a publicist at the age of 12, arranged by her parents, suggests that they have not discouraged her search for a new identity. Perhaps separating herself from her parents' hopes and dreams is difficult for her.

In her love life, she gives mixed messages. She made money from a tape of her sexual romps yet, at the same time, psychologically disassociated herself from her behaviour by claiming to have a low sex drive. She seems to be caught between her mask and her real self, unclear which direction to run in. She seems to use her sexy image as a provocative and powerful mask, but is in grave danger of becoming only known for that. She invites the audience to adore her as a sexual vamp, yet seems to feel trapped by this persona, wanting to be thought of, instead, as a nice person.

NOW ABOUT YOU

Find out: are you an extreme Exhibitionist?
If you answer yes to four or more of these questions, you may be an extreme Exhibitionist:

THE EXHIBITIONIST

1. Do you find it difficult to recognise how you are feeling?
2. Do you sometimes find it difficult to ask for what you want?
3. Do you have a tendency to hang on to destructive and painful relationships?
4. Did you have to take on adult responsibilities when you were a child?
5. Do you often feel insecure?
6. Do you find it difficult to trust people?
7. Do you sometimes feel that people don't really know who you are?
8. Do you sometimes feel trapped by your own behaviour?

WHY AM I AN EXTREME EXHIBITIONIST?

A combination of factors, including family influence and environment, can play their part in moulding this behaviour.

Family influences

You may have grown up in an environment with high instability, perhaps including an alcoholic or abusive parent, and therefore with no clear or consistent expectations, with no clear definition of appropriate behaviour.

Perhaps you also had a parent or parents who over-controlled you by telling you what to wear, when to speak or stay quiet, and who to have as friends. Alternatively, at the other extreme, they may have ignored you.

Did you learn early on how to squash your real feelings,

and place the needs of others first, for instance by taking on the role of emotional caretaker in the family? Or perhaps no one noticed if you were involved in risqué behaviour such as underage drinking, going out with older or inappropriate partners, or having underage sex. It's also possible that you developed a tough outer layer to deal with the world, so that no one could see how you were feeling, and that deep down you felt frustrated, angry, sad and insecure. And, as a consequence, you may now believe that you can't let people get close to you because they'll let you down, or you create an image of yourself that stops people getting close to you. Thinking like this can only lead to self-defeating behaviour.

THE POSITIVES AND NEGATIVES

Being an Exhibitionist gives you a wonderful mask to hide behind that can be incredibly powerful. Used positively, it can give you the courage to deal with some difficult situations. It can enable you to seem strong, when deep down inside you're shaking like a leaf.

But, used negatively, an extreme Exhibitionist can be a problem, and your mask might exclude people from your inner life. While you behave in an outrageous fashion, no one notices your vulnerability. In the past, your mask may have helped you to overcome shyness and feelings of insecurity but, at times, you may drink to excess, get very loud down at the pub and offer to kiss the first person who comes in the door.

If you are an Exhibitionist woman, you may dress in

THE EXHIBITIONIST

sexually provocative ways with a short skirt and low top to get people focusing on your physical side, while the more vulnerable you hides in the background. You may even meet someone for the first time, and before you know it open your heart and reveal your life story, and perhaps scare them off, leaving you thinking they're complete time-wasters. In particular, be wary of falling into the trap of thinking that relationships always go bad. Just consider the following case history.

Janine was on a blind date. She was excited about it, but also decided that she couldn't let this new man get to know her better because things always went wrong. Determined to keep him at arm's length, Janine put on her low-cut top and got out her razor-sharp tongue, and gave him hell. The result? He didn't call her back, and her belief that relationships always go wrong was reinforced.

What should I do if I'm like Janine?

Challenge your dominant mode of thought by asking the following questions:

1. Why do I think relationships will always go wrong when we've only just met? (And remember, in life there is no always.)
2. What signals am I sending out by the way I dress – one-night stand, or let's have a second date? And note, if they don't call back, was it because they thought I wasn't interested? After all, being sarcastic all evening isn't going to make the person think it's love, is it?

POSITIVE STEPS

Now let's look at another case history. Vicky came from a family where there were a lot of secrets. Her mum and dad split up when she was young, and her mum got together with someone new. Vicky's stepdad had a respectable job, was highly regarded in the community and seemed well grounded, but he had a big drink problem, which everyone in the family felt obliged to play down and deny.

Vicky learned how to cover for her stepdad, ringing up his office to say he was ill, even though he was actually upstairs in bed with a hangover. She became the rescuer in the family, lying to pretend all was well. Interestingly, when she started dating, she seemed to choose people who also had big problems, whether it was drink, a tendency to be physically abusive to her or being unpredictable. Her current partner hardly ever lets her know what time he'll be home, or where he is, and is secretive about his friends. She makes allowances for him all the time, and comforts herself with the thought that, underneath it all, he does respect her and he's kind and loving.

What should I do if I'm like Vicky?
First, be honest with yourself. If you are hiding behind the role of the rescuer and putting on your coping mask, then you have probably spent years carefully constructing it as a protective shield to hide behind. You may have spent a long time squashing your own emotions, and sometimes forgetting what you wanted. In many ways, it may have

THE EXHIBITIONIST

been easier to ignore any feelings of anger or frustration, instead focusing on the needs of others.

Stop. It's vital that you learn to notice and express your feelings (e.g. 'I'm really angry with him, he hasn't phoned to tell me where he is'). So record them in a diary. Don't ignore them. And, by doing this, you'll also start to recognise how your thoughts lead to certain feelings and repeated patterns of behaviour. Thus, if 'He threatened to hit me again. He seemed really sorry afterwards, and we had a nice cuddle. It my fault, because I don't realise how stressed he is' sounds familiar, think hard. When did stress ever mean that it's OK to hit someone? Seeing what you put up with in black-and-white terms will help you be honest with yourself.

Learn to build up your self-worth. You wear the mask to hide your vulnerabilities from yourself and those around you. Although it's helpful at first, it'll become a barrier to close bonds. Also, a strongly held belief that you're not getting attention unless you are taking care of someone else's needs leaves you feeling sad and lonely. That's why it's vital that you spend time without the mask.

So, spend just ten minutes each day without your mask on and ask yourself the following questions: does my choice of clothes make people think I'm unapproachable, a victim or fair game? And does walking with my head down and shoulders hunched signal that I'm low in confidence? Answer: of course it does, you're sending out the wrong signals. The more you practise dressing, speaking and behaving in a way that matches who you really are, the more you'll get the right responses.

CELEBRITY LIFE LAUNDRY

Learn to trust others, and develop a healthy network of friends. Part of the reason you may have developed this mask is that those close to you let you down. This may well have started in childhood when you were given the role of family caretaker and the guardian of secrets, and weren't allowed space to express frustration at being forced to be the grown-up or the one who told lies to safeguard secrets. You learned that what people said and what they actually did were two very different things. You had to learn to put the needs of others first, and minimise your feelings. Pretending became a way of life.

As a result, you may find it very difficult to tell the truth, or understand that others are telling the truth, possibly in time isolating yourself. This also means that people don't see the real you; they just see the role you play – the doormat or the outrageous mate.

It's therefore vital that you lose these stifling labels, and allow yourself to take small steps towards trusting people, by trying something new. If you normally shy away from spending intimate time with friends, then invite some round to your place for dinner. This will give you an opportunity to get to know others better.

Take care of yourself. If you were robbed of your childhood by having to grow up fast, having little love and instability, this might mean you're in danger of getting involved in destructive relationships – even with yourself.

A big step towards self-care is learning to ask what you need. It may be as simple as agreeing that a friend cooks

THE EXHIBITIONIST

you dinner when you feel unwell, or getting yourself a facial as a treat. It may involve learning to ditch people who aren't doing you any favours. Or it may mean seeking professional help from a therapist.

Avoid self-sabotage. Wearing a mask for so long is a bit like having a very close friend. Whenever you feel scared or insecure, you just call her up and she's there for you. However, a mask isn't the answer. It can be extremely damaging. Challenge the belief that you can't exist without it. Start recognising what makes you a competent person. Make a list of all your positive qualities ('I'm great at organising my time... I'm good at making friends...') and stick them on the wall. Read them every day, and stop relying on negative behaviour to get you attention.

CELEBRITY TIP

Use your strengths wisely. Pamela Anderson is adept at using her persona to draw attention to the causes she believes in. She may use her assets to gain maximum publicity for a cherished cause, while maintaining a degree of control about doing so, but ultimately she knows what she is doing and why. Understanding what makes you tick gives you control, and learning to use your strengths wisely gives you power, so use your voice positively.

CELEBRITY LIFE LAUNDRY

WHO EXHIBITIONISTS LOVE

Like a moth to a flame

In the past you've probably had no problems attracting people, whether it's because you are a brazen daredevil, or are amenable and a bit of a doormat. You put up such a front that people can't help but believe in the image you've given them. If you are in a relationship, you've probably already decided it won't last because all your relationships go wrong.

Dumped again

Sure enough, just as you've found yourself falling for someone, they appear to get bored and dump you – or, worse, abuse you and show you no respect.

Soul barer

As soon as you meet someone, you open your heart and bare your soul. They, in turn, seem to get scared and run in the opposite direction. This emotional splurging leaves you once again believing that you can't trust anyone because they'll let you down.

YOUR BIGGEST CHALLENGE

All things considered, your biggest challenge is letting go of some long-held beliefs about relationships. You may have had some bad experiences that reinforced your beliefs that you can't trust anyone, and that people always let you down. So take control and step back; it is

THE EXHIBITIONIST

vital to be honest about the signals you send out. Throwing out the 'script' that you are always going to be let down is crucial.

THE HEALTHY RELATIONSHIP FOR YOU

It's vital that you first focus on having a healthy relationship with yourself. Fear of intimacy may have held you back in the past. It's crucial that you resolve past hurts as your first important step. By identifying where your hurt comes from, you will start recognising your own feelings, and be able to express yourself more honestly. It may leave you feeling angry or sad at first, but also hugely released. By doing this, you'll open your eyes to the possibility of a healthy relationship. Only by doing this will you be able to recognise in others their positive, life-giving qualities. You'll be able to identify those who enjoy your company as you are, without the mask.

The right person for you won't take advantage of your vulnerabilities. They won't hurt you, or use sex as a way to keep you in check. And they won't play mind games with you, as you'll no longer be sending out confused signals. They'll be able to appreciate you as you are, and encourage you to drop the act and be yourself.

7
The Flamboyant Performer

You know just how to be a star. Those around you are dazzled by your pizzazz and fearlessness; centre stage holds no anxiety for you. It's the loss of the spotlight that causes you the greatest concern. In this chapter, we shall refer to this personality type as the Flamboyant Performer in order to embrace both its positive qualities and its challenging aspects.

Psychological research suggests that the fear of losing centre stage may have developed early on in childhood, and indicates that a child whose needs were not taken care of may have developed a 'smoke-screen' to deal with their difficult feelings. Perhaps, to cope with negative treatment, they may also have developed an over-inflated ego. This could result in the creation of their own world where all their needs are met, and where their demands can become increasingly unrealistic. According to psychologist Lynne Namka, this fantasy exists 'in order to build up a fragile self-esteem'. But the down side of not facing up to difficult feelings is the loss of closeness with others, and a lack of self-awareness.

THE FLAMBOYANT PERFORMER

If these defences go unchallenged, then people with such tendencies may develop faulty ways of thinking about themselves. They could become increasingly selfish and adept at imposing their wishes on others. In order to avoid pain, they might continually deny that they could be wrong and repress 'difficult' feelings. When these tendencies are not balanced, and become extreme, this type of thinking can create a person who is self-absorbed and devoid of empathy.

However, a more balanced Flamboyant Performer cannot only retain their larger-than-life appeal, and star quality, but also understand how to get their needs met appropriately, have the potential to give and take, and the ability to empathise with the needs of others.

Let's look at three Flamboyant Performer celebrities who exhibit the balanced and positive characteristics of this type.

SHARON STONE – THE SEDUCTIVE FLAMBOYANT PERFORMER

'I've got the biggest balls in Hollywood.' Sharon Stone

While other actresses were content to pose and flash pretty smiles on the red carpet at the 2006 Cannes Film Festival, Sharon Stone had other things on her mind. The star was in town for an event she never misses – playing auctioneer at an annual fundraiser for AIDS research. The actress and tireless charity campaigner danced on stage and boldly prodded the rich and famous to open up their pockets in order to set a new Cannes record by raising more than $4 million for research into the disease. The glittering annual event, organised by the Foundation for AIDS research (amFAR), has become one of the most highly sought-after parties at the Cannes Film Festival, with big companies buying up tables costing up to $100,000 each. Stone has become famous for being a relentless auctioneer, persuading the 700 guests to dig deep for charity and warning that 'Every six seconds someone dies.'

And Sharon's bold personality extends to all areas of her life. When her list of perks for starring in *Basic Instinct 2* emerged during the course of a lawsuit, it gave new meaning to the term 'Hollywood Diva'. She was in talks to reprise the role that made her famous – the no-knickers, ice-pick-wielding killer Catherine Tramell, but this time around she was a megastar, and wanted to be treated like one. In addition to her estimated £6.5-million salary, Sharon's typed list of requests made up a 26-point document – which ran to five pages – including demands for three full-time nannies for her son Roan, a Cadillac for her Pilates instructor, cars for her stylist and hairdresser, a full-time personal chef, 24-hour armed bodyguards and a convertible.

Sharon also required not one, but two full-time personal assistants. Further perks allegedly included seven first-class round-trip tickets for 'family, staff and companions' in the event of a private jet being unavailable, and a 'presidential hotel suite with two bedrooms'. Sharon also requested a total ban on cigar smoking on set, and stipulated that she was to keep all the clothes and jewellery she wore in the film. Oh, and lest

THE FLAMBOYANT PERFORMER

anyone forget who was the star, her name had to be as big as the film's title on all posters. If any other cast members appeared in any adverts, Sharon's likeness 'must also appear in substantially the same size as (or larger than) the other cast member.'

When asked about her demands, Sharon simply replied, 'When women stand up for their rights or want to achieve something in the world, they are usually called bad names. When men [do the same], they are called thoughtful, level-headed, confident figureheads. Interestingly enough, I was called bad names and I achieved things.'

And, as one of the most sought-after and well-recognised faces in the world today, Sharon Stone has certainly done that.

> Crew members on *Diabolique* criticised Sharon for her entourage of ten to twelve assistants, including her own make-up person, personal trainer, driver and bodyguards, all making demands on her behalf. Beth Goetz, a parent of one of the children in the film, told one paper about her experience with Sharon. 'She was a very nice person, but she had a very colourful vocabulary. One day she really did use foul language. She fell down the steps. She's lying there yelling, "Fan me, fan me," and there are people going, "Yes, Miss Stone." She said, "I'm not going to continue shooting unless you air-condition this (expletive) building." She didn't watch her language a lot around the kids.'

Sharon Stone was dubbed worst celebrity interview by GMTV's Carla Romano. According to Carla, it started off well – she says she thoroughly enjoyed her interview with Stone until she made the mistake of asking what it was like to be single again. 'She whipped her head round and barked at the cameraman, "Stop the tape!"' says Romano. 'Then she turned back to me. "Get out!" she snarled. My instinct was to laugh. She struck me as ridiculous.'

According to E! online columnist Ted Casablancas, in December 2005 Sharon Stone did a photo shoot at a major fashion studio in LA. Sharon was posing for French *Vogue* and, according to studio spies, the star actress insisted on entering through the rear, not allowing her name to be printed on the studio's daily call sheet and not communicating with studio staffers.

While shooting *Basic Instinct 2* in London, there were reports that Sharon had hired a personal food taster – an aide whose full-time job was to sample food before it passed over Sharon's lips. According to *Mail on Sunday* columnist Katie Nichol, 'Her taster trawled organic food shops to test products she was interested in. Then Sharon made a second visit to quiz staff about colourings, hydrogenated fat, flavourings and preservatives. She eats only the best foods.'

Equally colourful tales leaked out from the set of *Catwoman*. There were allegations that Sharon demanded last-minute script changes, walked off set

THE FLAMBOYANT PERFORMER

> during shooting to make phone calls, and demanded better furnishings in her trailer. It was claimed that members of the crew used to exchange anecdotes about Sharon's diva-like behaviour each day. Whoever had the best 'Sharon Stone story' would be treated to free drinks all night. And such antics have not been confined to her professional life. On a flight to London recently, she reportedly grabbed a stewardess's attention by screaming, 'Hey, girlie! Girlie!' and then insisted the first-class toilet be reserved solely for her use.

Sharon's current status as a superstar is a far cry from her first job in a small-town McDonald's. She was born one of four children in Meadville, Pennsylvania, to factory worker Joseph and Avon lady Dorothy. After an IQ test early in her life revealed astonishing intelligence, she was urged to become a lawyer. But for the girl obsessed with Fred Astaire and Ginger Rogers films, there was never any doubt about her goals: she wanted to be a movie star. 'I was going to be a star even if I had lived under a hay pile in Idaho,' she said. 'It was part of my destiny.'

She was the nerdy one of the family, but her early years were marked by ambition. When the duckling turned swan, she realised that she could use her looks to make her fortune. 'I didn't even get asked to my prom,' she said. 'Now the entire world thinks I'm sexy.'

Yet it was not an easy journey. Sharon started out winning beauty pageants and from there she became a Ford model. Her big break came when Woody Allen cast her in a bit part in his film *Stardust Memories*. After a decade and a string of B-list movies, Sharon landed a role in *Total Recall* alongside Arnold Schwarzenegger at the age of 32. She capitalised on this with a ten-page spread in *Playboy*, which led to the role of a lifetime in *Basic Instinct*.

As she became successful, Sharon made sure she took care of her family. 'We didn't have a luxurious upbringing, but now [my parents have] got round-the-clock staff, and the cook, and the work-out person, and the massage person. They've accepted the burden of luxury quite easily – they don't have the big price tag [that goes with celebrity]. But my dad worked swing shifts in a factory when we were kids, and drove an hour to work each day.' She tells a story about getting a new dress for a school dance, and suddenly realising that her mother wore a shoe with a hole in it so that she could afford to buy the dress for Sharon.

Despite being 48 years old – an age in Hollywood when most actresses find that the only roles available are playing mother to a young ingénue – Sharon's fearless flamboyancy once again made its impact in *Basic Instinct 2*. 'I felt we should hold off on the full nudity for a while in [*Basic Instinct 2*] and then I thought that when I ultimately did do the nude scene it should be done in a startling way that would be disturbing and threatening,' she told London's *Evening Standard*. 'By the time the film is released, I will be 48 and I wanted to do the nudity in a way that's quite brazen. I wanted her to be very masculine, like a man in a steam room, and I wanted the audience to have a moment where they realise she's naked and then realise she's a forty-something woman and naked.'

THE FLAMBOYANT PERFORMER

Sharon's private life has never been boring. Her five-year marriage to newspaper editor Phil Bronstein, also known as 'El Macho' because of his fiery temper, ended in 2003. Since that time, the stunning star has been seen out with a varied array of handsome, successful men.

Tales of Sharon's diva-like behaviour are plentiful. When *GQ* magazine asked her to pose for a cover, it was reported that Sharon would only be photographed wearing a Vera Wang zebra-striped jumpsuit, and it was Sharon's idea that she would pose between two live zebras. *GQ* tried to oblige, but apparently had a hard time coming up with the animals. It was reported that Sharon lost out on the coveted cover shot and *GQ* went with Ben Affleck instead. And then there was her very public battle with jeweller-to-the-stars Harry Winston. She borrowed a $600,000 diamond necklace to wear to the Oscars, and afterwards insisted that it had been a gift to her. One $12-million lawsuit and a whole lot of name-calling later, Winston finally got his diamonds back – and Sharon's diva reputation was further cemented.

Despite stories to the contrary, Stone insists she has mellowed since suffering a brain aneurysm in 2001. 'It was the best thing that ever happened to me. I found my humanity,' she insisted.

There are a host of significant ways in which Sharon Stone has used the sheer force of her personality to do incredible good. The actress has worked tirelessly raising money at celebrity events for AIDS research and has been deeply involved with America's largest charity for HIV research, amFAR, for nearly 20 years. While attending the World Economic Forum, she stole the show at a session on saving children in Africa from malaria by standing up and announcing, 'I'm Sharon Stone. I was particularly moved by President Mkapa and by his urgent need of today, so, if you don't mind, I would like to offer you $10,000 to help you buy some [anti-mosquito] nets today. Would anyone else like to be on a team with me and stand up and offer some money?'

The chairman of the meeting, American senator Bill Frist, asked her to sit down. But one by one, the suited businessmen rose and made pledges. Five minutes later, Frist spoke again: 'Sharon, you got $1 million already.'

Although she is most famous as a sex symbol, Sharon has channelled her strength of character to do good for others, in a way that only she can. Ultimately, Sharon Stone is unapologetic about her attitude, saying, 'If you have a vagina and an attitude in this town, then it's a lethal combination.' And fast approaching 50, she shows no signs of mellowing. 'Like a great Bordeaux, I just keep getting better.'

Analyse this: Sharon Stone

Sharon certainly exudes star quality. She is good at self-promotion and excels at being a sensation. However, some of her behaviour reveals the Flamboyant Performer brooding just beneath the surface. When asked about her diva-esque demands, she switches the focus of attention and finds someone else to blame.

The actress also appears to use those around her to maintain the veneer that she is very special. And by

THE FLAMBOYANT PERFORMER

wanting superior treatment on a flight, changing scripts to suit her or at times becoming aggressive, she demonstrates that she thinks it important that everyone acknowledges her powerful position. But perhaps this betrays a more fragile ego. That powerful outer layer – a sexy woman, a woman who demands the best things in life – may well mask a more fragile person underneath who may fear that without all the star trappings she is not that important. Sharon reflects the more balanced Flamboyant Performer – a terrific achiever and, through her charity work, one able to empathise with the needs of others.

SHARON OSBOURNE – THE POLISHED FLAMBOYANT PERFORMER

'Talk about going down. Have you got something stuck in the back of your throat?'
Sharon Osbourne to Celebrity X Factor contestant Rebecca Loos

Perched in her chair on the set of the London studio of ITV's *X Factor* sits a slim, glamorous woman with stylishly coiffed hair and the creamy skin of someone half her age. The glittering diamonds on her neck sparkle as she makes another outrageous comment that sends the audience into spasms of delight. This is Sharon Osbourne, mother of three, rock-star royalty and one of the UK's most loved Flamboyant Performers.

At 53, Sharon Osbourne has become a global brand, with a profile so high it almost eclipses that of her famous husband. In the last few years, this formerly overweight mum has transformed herself through cosmetic surgery, shed more than 9st and filled her extensive wardrobe with designer clothing. There are no more oversized knitted sweaters in this lady's closet.

It's a great time to be Sharon Osbourne. Her children are now grown up and, despite the fact that both Kelly and Jack have done stints in drug rehab, they now seem to be well adjusted and close to their parents. Ozzy is well and truly sober and more devoted to his wife than ever, and Sharon herself recently triumphed over a frightening bout of colon cancer.

Professionally, it seems that all she touches turns to gold. When she agreed to allow cameras into her Beverly Hills family home, MTV suddenly had its most successful reality-TV show ever. But that was just the beginning for Sharon, who was soon the face every editor wanted on the cover of their glossy magazine, while tabloid readers lapped up headlines about 'Shazza'. Then came her role as the sometimes sweet and always direct judge on the break-out hit *The X Factor*, and her bestselling biography, appropriately titled *Extreme*. The new and improved Sharon is now earning dizzyingly astronomical pay cheques, shows up on red carpets around the globe and is courted by top-end firms to front national ad campaigns. As she once put it, 'Isn't it amazing that so much can happen in our lives? I've had the drama and then, boom! Something even more dramatic happens, and you think, my God. "Everything in moderation" – it should be – but unfortunately, moderation has not been a part of my life in any other way.'

THE FLAMBOYANT PERFORMER

Sharon's love for the outrageous extends to her passion for shopping. She enjoys indulging herself and those she loves, and is frequently spotted lugging around designer carrier bags. Regular viewers of *The Osbournes* will recall the affection that Sharon lavishes on her coterie of miniature dogs (she pays for their teeth to be whitened), who are often found sleeping in her bed or cuddled in her arms during an interview. Her love of the high life also includes her collection of hundreds of designer handbags, thousands of pounds' worth of jewels, as well as the comfort of a live-in staff with a private jet at her beck and call.

Part of Sharon's undeniable appeal as a Flamboyant Performer, much like Elton John and Sharon Stone, lies in her seemingly unstoppable urge to say exactly what is on her mind. Who could forget her outburst on national television about actress Nicole Kidman: 'She needs a good meal, a sandwich, that's what she needs. Skinny cow, she is!' Despite her own fondness for going under the knife, Sharon also took superstar Melanie Griffith to task on the subject: 'Melanie Griffith has destroyed herself. She was this lovely, fresh, blonde Californian girl and now she's just grotesque.' And Hollywood legends don't escape her wrath either: 'Mickey Rourke – God! He obviously hates himself.' She also let the insults fly at Michael Douglas: 'Another terrible face job. Poor old twat.' Sharon even took a swipe at Madonna: 'She is so full of shit. I would like to punch her. She's into Kabbalah one minute, she's a Catholic the next. She'll be a Hindu soon, no doubt.' But why stop there? She also managed to cram a few other names into her binge of scorn: 'Who else? Oh yes, Bono. What a twat. And Diana Ross. Awful woman.'

Sharon's physical transformation seems to play a big role in her confidence. Her once frumpy-and-dumpy image is now long gone; and she has spoken frankly about the endless plastic surgery she has undergone. She has admitted to having liposuction on her neck, and a 'neck lift'. She also had her breasts lifted, liposuction on her arms, her tummy tucked, her bottom lifted and implants inserted. 'And I had my legs lifted. Yes, I love cosmetic surgery,' she once said proudly. 'I've had everything done – my whole face. I've had my arms, my boobs, my stomach, my bum and my legs done.' Sharon confessed to spending a staggering amount to change her appearance – £120,000 to date, even with regular nip-and-tucker discounts. 'The boobs were cheap – he gave me a special rate of £12,000 because I'm such a good customer.' And was it worth it? 'Ozzy does like my new tits. A lot. He loves them, actually.'

No one is more surprised by her extraordinary success than Sharon herself. 'I am a working mum. I've always been a working mum. A few years ago, before we moved to America, I was one of those mums who would drive the kids to school, do my work, come back, pick up the kids and do dinner. I never expected to become famous like this,' she says. 'At my age? No, never. For it to come so late in life? Never in a million years.'

Despite her superstar status, Sharon swears she is still the same woman. 'I am just me – nothing has changed.

THE FLAMBOYANT PERFORMER

I'm still Ozzy's wife,' she says. 'I am definitely not a star. I am something of a celebrity, but I am not a star. A star for what? I can't bloody do anything. And I don't have a stylist. Surely anyone at fucking 53 can dress themselves? Right or wrong, I choose all my clothes and my hair is done by cousin Terry. I am not bloody Madonna.'

Sharon was not always this confident. She struggled with weight problems as a teenager and visited her first health farm at the age of 15. As a teenager, she was not popular with boys and described herself as short, fat and hairy. After years spent fighting to shed extra weight, Sharon had a gastric banding procedure, in which an elastic band is put around the stomach. Within a year, she had gone from 16st to just 7st. It took a while for her to get used to her stunning new looks. 'The moment I realised everything really had changed was when a magazine put me in its list of the 50 most beautiful women in 2002. I had never ever considered myself beautiful. That word was never used for me except by Ozzy, but he loved me, so I could never accept it.'

In addition to her weight, Sharon Osbourne faced other struggles growing up. The daughter of music producer Don Arden, she was raised in a house in Brixton that was perpetually filled with a variety of music stars. Her relationship with her mother was strained, to say the least. As Sharon says, 'She didn't like me, she didn't give a shit. But I didn't like her either.'

Sharon went to work for the family business while still in her teens. She soon began dating Ozzy Osbourne, one of her dad's clients, and married him in 1982, taking over his management in the process. This caused a massive rift in the family. In fact, after this Sharon's dad did not speak to his daughter for 20 years. They are reconciled now, but Sharon never saw her mother again (she died in the late 1990s).

> *X Factor* talent-show judge Sharon Osbourne made headlines for her vitriolic comments about *Celebrity X Factor* contestant Rebecca Loos. Sharon was unapologetic about her biting remarks to the woman who claims to have been David Beckham's mistress, vowing, 'I won't stop and I won't change my views. More power to Rebecca for coming back and taking the abuse. But I don't respect her one ounce. You can't respect her. I don't know why she's still here. It must be the men's vote. I don't know why one woman in the country would stand up and say they like her other than her mother.'
>
> According to a UK survey, Sharon Osbourne is the most successful reinvented star. The *X Factor* host and wife of rock star Ozzy is reported to have spent £120,000 on plastic surgery. Sharon has had liposuction, tummy tucks, breast lifts, bottom lifts and a face lift. A national poll found that many dissatisfied Brits are desperate to change identity. If money was no object, six in ten would fork out £0.5 million to reinvent themselves as their favourite celebs. Michael Jackson was voted as having the most disastrous change.

THE FLAMBOYANT PERFORMER

> In early June 2006, Sharon Osbourne reportedly stormed off *Celebrity X Factor* after a furious row with fellow judge Simon Cowell. A show insider told the *Mirror*, 'Sharon just left the studio. Her daughter Kelly was waiting for her and had no idea she'd gone. It was all kicking off – producers were trying to persuade Sharon to do the *Xtra Factor* with the other judges but she wouldn't budge. She felt truly let down by Simon and just didn't want to be around him. For him to choose to get rid of her act after failing to back her up was just too much. She was incandescent and had to get out of the studio before it all got out of hand.'

There have also been years of turmoil: she has put her husband and two of her three children through rehab, recovered from cancer, had £2 million of jewellery snatched from her Buckinghamshire home, nursed Ozzy back to health after a near-fatal accident on a quad bike and fought her own battles with binge-eating and bulimia. Sharon recently confessed that she has tried seeing a counsellor for a course of heavy-duty Freudian therapy. When asked why, she responds, 'Loads of reasons. I am very fucked up. I'm seriously fucked up. There are a lot of things I am very mixed up about. Eating. My weight. Overspending. And I have terrible, terrible guilt all the time. About everything.'

Like a lot of balanced Flamboyant Performers, Sharon has used her exceptional star power to raise money for a good cause. Her battle with cancer led her to found the Sharon Osbourne Colon Cancer Program at the Cedars-Sinai Medical Center in Los Angeles. She comments, 'I started it because I had so much help while I was going through my cancer treatment – they have such a great support group. But during that time I saw so many other people with cancer who were going through it on their own. It was then that I thought if I make it I want to give something back.'

Her outspoken candour may shock and surprise, but, for her fans, her occasionally foul-mouthed and unpredictable rants are part of what makes her so lovable. The best thing about Sharon Osbourne is that she is truly unique: we should only get worried if she starts acting like everyone else.

Analyse this: Sharon Osbourne

Sharon has blossomed through reinvention, and has made no secret of how she has achieved her fame and fortune. But step away from the obvious external changes and you uncover a strong, outspoken survivor who has been through a wide range of experiences, some of them deeply painful. Her roller-coaster life unveils a woman growing from invisibility to high-profile visibility – these extreme highs and lows, and her ability to circumnavigate them, make her a balanced Flamboyant Performer.

But how has this happened? Sharon admits to a difficult relationship with her mother, and has explained that she felt she didn't get attention from either of her parents. It seems as though Sharon's mother and father

THE FLAMBOYANT PERFORMER

were focused elsewhere, and as we have seen she herself described that she felt her own mother didn't like her. Perhaps her parents were focused more on their own needs and wants, leaving her to find her own ways to survive and deal with the situation. Research suggests that children whose needs are consistently ignored and neglected may well develop a tough outer layer to cope with the world, and protect themselves from further hurt. It seems too that Sharon had to devise ways to win her parents' approval, something any child craves. Perhaps she found her role within the family by being charming and shrewd, and playing a supporting role to her powerful father; winning his attention in this way may have made her feel good about herself.

In her marriage, Sharon continued to play a supporting and supportive role to Ozzy the rock star and her children, whether it was shouldering difficulties, painful illness or being an accomplished businesswoman. But she gradually moved from the shadows to take front stage, to show the world the full force of her star quality.

Like the balanced Flamboyant Performer that she is, Sharon admits to being self-indulgent, and at times outrageous – certainly not someone afraid to take centre stage. But this is tempered by being aware of her own limitations, as well as an enormous capacity for empathy in her support of good causes and raising money and awareness for charities.

CELEBRITY LIFE LAUNDRY

ELTON JOHN – THE REBELLIOUS FLAMBOYANT PERFORMER

> 'The great thing about rock'n'roll is that someone like me can be a star.' Elton John

At the Chopard party in the South of France, nervous party organisers paced the room. Sir Elton John had been trumpeted as the honoured guest on dozens of press releases and the delighted sponsors had draped him in more than 120 carats of diamond jewellery for the bash. But something had happened inside. The flamboyant singer was on stage before the main event to present the Chopard Trophy to one of his favourite actors, Kevin Zegers. All went according to plan, until an overzealous photographer interrupted his speech while he was praising the young actor's film *Transamerica*. Annoyed with the overeager snapper's loud demand to smile for the cameras, John leaned into his microphone, and said sternly, 'If you saw *Transamerica*... I'm talking... you fuckwit, fucking photographers, you should be shot, you should all be shot. Thank you.' Elton then passed off the trophy to Kevin with the comment, 'They are a fucking nightmare,' and returned to his seat. He left shortly afterwards.

It was just the latest temperamental outburst from one of the world's most flamboyant stars. In the TV documentary *Tantrums and Tiaras* made about him by filmmaker (and partner) David Furnish, Sir Elton was shown storming off a tennis court after a woman called out 'yoo-hoo' at him. While fleeing, he was heard to mutter, 'I'm never coming back to the South of France

THE FLAMBOYANT PERFORMER

again.' In fact, he's quite good at letting rip. He once berated Madonna for lip-synching and George Michael for being too reclusive, and called photographers at Taiwan airport 'rude, vile pigs'.

Despite these ill-tempered rants, Sir Elton is also viewed as one of the most generous and lavish entertainers in the world. He certainly knows how to throw a party, and regularly manages to out-glitz all other entertainment moguls with his Oscar-night party. In 2006, his lavish party at the Pacific Design Center in West Hollywood attracted the biggest names in showbiz. Sharon Stone, Tim Allen, Pamela Anderson, Paris Hilton, Lindsay Lohan, Lisa Snowdon, Sharon and Ozzy Osbourne and a host of other stars were treated to musical performances by their legendary host with Grammy award-winner John Legend and, when the pair launched into a duet of 'Rocket Man', the entire crowd joined in. The guests drained thousands of dollars' worth of champagne (both the vintage and the pink varieties), mojitos and martinis. Even the reclusive singer Prince was spotted boogying on the dance floor. The event was not simply a great party, though – Elton had an agenda. That night raised more than £2 million for his AIDS Foundation charity. The Oscar after-party epitomises Elton's spirit: he is a megastar whose love of the high life is legendary, yet he uses his standing and talent to raise millions for a good cause.

There is no denying that Elton John has got where he is today because of his sheer musical genius. The piano-playing singer has recorded instantly recognisable songs such as 'Rocket Man', 'Someone Saved My Life Tonight' and 'Your Song'. He has scored award-winning musical hits such as *The Lion King* and *Billy Elliott*. His musical career spans more than 30 years and he has accumulated a fortune estimated at about £175 million. Elton also has a knighthood and lavish homes in London, Windsor, Venice, Nice and Atlanta. He recently married long-time partner David, has achieved global fame and remains a superstar after three decades in the business.

> Sir Elton John accepted £100,000 libel damages from the *Daily Mail* in the High Court in May 2006 over allegations that he issued a 'bizarre and absurd edict' to guests at his annual charity ball ordering them not to approach him during the event.
>
> The star's solicitor-advocate Nigel Tait told Mr Justice Eady in the High Court, 'In fact, not only was no such edict issued at all, Sir Elton greets each guest as they arrive.'
>
> Sir Elton used the money for a good cause – he donated all of the damages to the Elton John AIDS Foundation.

Elton was born Reginald Kenneth Dwight on 25 March 1947, in the London suburb of Pinner. Music was a part of his life from early on: his father, an RAF officer, played the trumpet, and Elton learned to play the piano at a young age. His promise led to a scholarship to the Royal Academy of Music, but there he realised that his heart

THE FLAMBOYANT PERFORMER

belonged not to the classics, but to rock'n'roll – he idolised Ray Charles, Chuck Berry and Buddy Holly. After playing at local hotels, he joined a band, Bluesology, in 1961 aged just 14 (he became Elton John by combining names of two other band members).

His life transformed forever when he met Bernie Taupin, a then unknown writer from Lincolnshire. Elton released his debut album, *Empty Sky*, in June 1969, and he and Bernie have proved an unstoppable hit machine ever since.

However, Elton's musical odyssey has not been accompanied by an equally smooth emotional ride. He has spoken candidly about the fact that his father could not understand his son's drive to become a musician, and, to this day, Elton believes that this conflict led to his lifelong struggle with low self-esteem: 'I just thought I could never do anything right in my father's eyes. He just intimidated me so much. I was afraid of him big-time. I used to think I could never do anything right. I know it knocked my self-esteem and I still suffer from that all the time. I still have terrible problems with the way I look, with my weight and stuff like that.'

According to Elton, his low self-confidence triggered well-documented battles with booze, drugs and binge eating. Elton struggled with an addiction to cocaine and alcohol for much of his career, although he has now been sober for more than a decade. Today, his friends say he is compassionate and generous, yet he remains impetuous and volatile. 'I know I'll never take cocaine again,' he insists, 'but the other things – the rage and the temper and, I think, the irrationality – are still there. But it's part of being creative. There are still times, especially when I'm tired, when the bad temper and the irrationality come out. And I hate that. The chink in my armour is still there. I don't seem to have anger, I have rage. I would love to have the ability to rationalise something and talk things through. I can't. I'm very emotional. Being unreasonably emotional makes me feel like I've had a line of coke or something.'

He once recounted an incident that took place at Elizabeth Hurley's Chelsea house after she'd given birth to her son, Damian. Elton was there with partner David. Liz couldn't get out of her house because there were hundreds of photographers outside, which made Elton lose his temper big time: 'It was what I said to them. The venom that comes out,' he says. 'It's a bit like something out of *The Exorcist*.'

Despite his battle to accept himself, or perhaps because of it, Elton enjoys an outrageously lavish lifestyle. Visiting his mansion in Nice, one reporter noted, 'Walking through Elton's closet is like a tour of Versailles – splendour, magnificence and order. Row after row of white tennis shoes sit upright on foot spikes like pristine, obedient soldiers standing to attention. Silk Versace robes hang unwrinkled. He heads up another flight of stairs to the TV room, which has a 360-degree view of Nice and a massive skylight.' His prolific approach to consumption is perfectly summed up by a sign on the kitchen wall in his Windsor mansion. It reads: 'Of course I need it today. If I wanted it tomorrow, I'd order it tomorrow.'

THE FLAMBOYANT PERFORMER

Today, Elton has certainly learned to channel his energy and vision in a positive direction, and now directs his passions towards helping people. In 1991, he established the Elton John AIDS Foundation, his pioneering charity dedicated to breakthrough work on behalf of those around the world suffering from HIV and related illnesses. In 2005, he candidly spoke of the moment he wept with joy when he was invited to perform at the Live 8 concert. He insists that, today, he understands the full meaning of this event compared to the way he felt about taking part in Live Aid 20 years ago, when he was a 'self-obsessed drug addict' who never really appreciated the importance of the cause. 'I have been sober and clean for 15 years,' Elton said, 'and I think I have grown up and matured a bit. I'm honoured to play at this concert because it means more to me now than it did then.'

Analyse this: Elton John

Elton John certainly seems to embody the classic signs of the Flamboyant Performer. By his own admission, he behaves as though he deserves special treatment. On the one hand, he recognises that his demands are outrageous, but, on the other, he seems to crave attention and to be placated, like a child who wants to be comforted by its parents.

The clearest indications of why Elton may behave this way seem to stem from his childhood and what appears to have been a rather emotionally distant father. Although Elton worked hard to gain his dad's approval and understanding, his father seemed to remain hard to please. It is possible that Elton had to hide his true feelings from his dad and work overtime to please him. A child in this tremendously difficult position may start to create an inflated and false self as protection against further pain. The child may then develop a tough outer layer to hide the more scared and fragile self and, of course, this needs fierce protecting and explains why any criticism is taken extremely badly.

At times, as an adult, Elton has by his own admission been very critical and judgemental of those around him but, at the same time, has seemed to suffer terrible emotional wounding if he feels that he himself has been ill treated. In the past, he has resorted to destructive behaviour, including taking drugs and bingeing on alcohol, perhaps to deal with emotional difficulties and negative feelings about himself. These are key features of someone experiencing the negative effects of being a Flamboyant Performer.

Elton is exacting in his work yet chaotic with his money. This is another feature of the Flamboyant Performer, characterised by Elton simultaneously being the star of the show while feeling driven to behave extravagantly to fulfil his own special status, to soothe his fragile self-esteem.

He seems to have developed a deeper understanding of his emotions and how they are affecting him, and it's this self-awareness – and the awareness of others, reflected in his enduring relationship with David, as well as his generous charity work – that has created a more balanced outlook and approach in his life.

THE FLAMBOYANT PERFORMER

NOW ABOUT YOU

Find out: are you a Flamboyant Performer?
Answer the following questions. If you answer yes to more than four, then you might be a Flamboyant Performer:

1. Did you learn early in childhood to bring success to your parents as a way to gain their attention?
2. Did you learn to be extra special to please your parents?
3. Do you have problems forming and keeping close relationships?
4. Do you feel wounded if someone points out a fault of yours?
5. Do you find it hard to empathise with other people's feelings?
6. Do you often feel anxious or agitated if you are not the centre of attention?
7. Do you find that you are often very judgemental of other people?
8. Do you often feel that you are entitled to special treatment?

WHY AM I A FLAMBOYANT PERFORMER?

The key influences are as follows:
Research indicates that children whose emotional needs are ignored may develop strong defences against further hurt, shame or fear. They do this by developing a false self to cope with the world, and to guard against feelings of

inferiority. Therefore, they may learn to protect their fragile egos with a superiority complex. This could involve bragging about material wealth – for example showing off to other people that they have the best car, the best clothes or whatever makes them feel better.

If you are a Flamboyant Performer, perhaps you worked very hard to gain your parents' attention. Perhaps this was because you had parents who were selfishly wrapped up in their own importance. You may have seen them bossing other people around, or claiming that other people were idiots.

You may now be very good at being a star at work, and on the surface very charming, as long as you are getting attention. You may experience a desperate need for admiration, and have fantasies of greatness and self-importance. However, if denied, you may believe that this is a personal affront and an insult. You may resort to becoming aggressive, or having outbursts, to cope with the difficult feelings of rejection or shame. If this is you, then one of your most powerful central sentiments is: 'I'm special, how could you do this to me?'

The flamboyant Performer carries within it both a gift and a burden. On the positive side, you know exactly how to get attention, to be a star and glory in it. But the problem is, the complex can hurt. When you are not the centre of attention, you feel devalued. As a result, you struggle with feelings of frustration, anger and even depression when you think that you are not being given special treatment. Underneath it all, you may feel desperately insecure, fearful, ashamed and very small,

THE FLAMBOYANT PERFORMER

and therefore work very hard to hide this unpalatable side of yourself by going to the other extreme, and over-inflating your importance.

Let's go one step further. Read the following case history.

Emma was trying on clothes at an exclusive boutique. She went into the changing room with armfuls of clothes, which was against the rules, but pleaded that she didn't have much time and had to try things on quickly. The sales assistant reluctantly let her have her way, and did everything she could to help. She got Emma alternative sizes, colours and styles, none of which met her approval. She simply didn't like anything. In the end, Emma dumped all the clothes in a heap on the floor, complaining that the boutique was useless and the assistant had been most unhelpful.

The result? The reinforced belief that she deserved better treatment, that the store was rubbish and that other people were to blame.

What should I do if I'm like Emma?

Think about what really happened in the boutique. What was your increasing anger really all about? Rather than point the finger of blame, ask yourself:

> *Did I really have enough time to find the perfect outfit during my lunch hour?*
> *Was I expecting the store to know what I wanted without really having a clue what I was looking for myself?*
> *Was I getting angry with the sales assistant when*

CELEBRITY LIFE LAUNDRY

really I was annoyed with myself for leaving it too late to buy an outfit?

By examining your behaviour, you will come to appreciate the errors in your thinking. Blaming others made you feel better, but who was really responsible for things not working out? Yes – you.

Now consider this next case history. Fran came from a wonderful family. She went on fabulous family holidays, wore the best clothes and ate out with her parents at the best restaurants. Her friends at school were green with envy. She had everything money could buy. But, whenever she wanted her mum or dad to take notice of something she'd done, or to help her deal with an emotional problem, they simply gave her some cash, and told her to go out and make herself happy.

Fran learned to sideline her feelings and throw money at her problems. As an adult, she became addicted to shopping and showing off her goodies to her friends. She never wanted to hear about her friends' problems, and often turned conversations back to herself when she got bored. Her friends nicknamed her the 'What-about-me-girl?', but then stopped calling her, or inviting her out to parties. Fran simply wrote them off as useless, but she couldn't escape the nagging guilt at spending money, or the hurt at being left by herself. Not able to face up to these difficult feelings, she went shopping again, and fell into even deeper debt.

THE FLAMBOYANT PERFORMER

What should I do if I'm like Fran?
Examine the past. One of the hardest things for you to do is understand your past, and examining the past carefully hurts. OK, the past cannot be changed, but the future can. In order to free yourself of pain and disappointment, it's vital that you understand what caused them. Keeping a diary will help you develop a picture. Ask yourself...

> *When I was a child, were my emotional needs met?*
> *How did I feel when my needs were ignored?*
> *How did I learn to disguise my hurts?*

Learn to listen to others. The biggest challenge you have is empathising with other people's feelings. Because you feel so special, and feel that you need to protect yourself from the world, it's very hard for you to recognise other people's social cues. You may be desperately trying to protect your fragile self from being hurt, but your defensive behaviour may mean that you end up being rude, aggressive or dismissive.

A wonderful start to achieving this is to learn to stand in someone else's shoes. Put simply, when you encounter someone socially, or at work, instead of endlessly talking about yourself and inflating your importance at their expense, learn to ask them simple questions such as 'How are you?' It seems so basic, but it will be met with a warmer response and less hostility than your own self-centred chatter. It will also show the other person that you care.

Stop being a critic. You believe that you are right and make the wrong assumption that, if something goes wrong, it is someone else's fault. No one likes to be continuously blamed, and you have a habit of pointing the finger at everyone but yourself. You may do this to make yourself feel better. The irony is, you need people to praise you and make you feel important, yet at the same time you abuse those same people for not meeting your very high expectations of them. Remember, behaving badly can leave you lonely and isolated.

You may not clearly understand why your friendships are short term and tense. So, starting to pierce your own bubble is a positive step. Rather than continuing with a faulty idea – I'm right, and they are useless – challenge yourself by saying, 'I need to consider my part in what went wrong.'

Be realistic. You may go out and buy all the latest designer clothes because you strongly believe you must have the best and most expensive – after all, you deserve the best. You keep getting letters from the bank telling you that you are overdrawn. But, instead of confronting your problems, you ignore the bills. This needs to stop. Living in a fantasy is damaging. Take a reality check. Ask yourself, is wearing the best clothes really that satisfying? Shouldn't this debt frighten you?

Ask for help. One of your biggest defences is wanting to believe that you are very special. You may maintain this position by operating as though you are better than everybody else. But continuing like this means that you'll never recognise and deal with your own pain. There are good reasons why you may have developed these self-protective defences. However, you may also be alienating those around you, and alienating you from yourself.

THE FLAMBOYANT PERFORMER

Dealing with difficult feelings is the key to breaking out of your fantasy world, where you are the only special one.

In order to break through, you have to break down. Working with a therapist may be another key step to dealing safely with distressing feelings. You'll understand the emotions that underlie your need to be special. But you have to admit to yourself, first, that you need help, and, second, that there is someone who can help you.

> **CELEBRITY TIP**
>
> Over the years, Elton John has improved his sense of self-awareness. He has been able to confront some of his behaviour and successfully worked hard to own up to his own outbursts. When you don't get what you want, you may resort to dramatic and childlike outbursts, bear grudges, feel vengeful or get aggressive. When you are in the grip of this rage, you see the world through very narrow lenses. By doing so, you may be projecting your anger on to others. This is a self-defeating strategy, and means that you may spend a lifetime stuck in this mindset – and being very lonely as a result.
>
> So, take a long, deep breath before you blow your top. This will give you a chance to cool off, and analyse what has happened. It sounds simple, but by doing this you will reduce the risk of an outburst that you will later regret.

CELEBRITY LIFE LAUNDRY

THE FLAMBOYANT PERFORMER IN LOVE

Three main ideas crop up repeatedly in the relationships of Flamboyant Performers:

The accessory
In the past, you may have found that your relationships didn't last very long. One reason for this might have been that you saw your lovers as an extension of yourself. They were there to soothe you and meet your very high demands. You treated them as property. Positioning yourself so centrally in relationships meant that your lovers felt ignored.

I'm perfect, you're faulty
Perhaps in the past when things went wrong, you blamed the other person, and rather than face up to difficult or uncomfortable ideas – like 'Maybe it was me' – you ran away and looked for someone else to feed you emotionally.

Looking-glass love
You may have chosen someone just like you, and enjoyed this 'looking-glass love'; it may have made you feel safe because they mirrored your beliefs and behaviour. But the similarities would have caused tension as both of you vied for the number-one spot, and this would have been unbearable for both parties.

So, your biggest challenge is to empathise and pick up on the feelings of your partner. Running away from relationship difficulties means that for you intimacy is

THE FLAMBOYANT PERFORMER

very hard to achieve. Seeing your lover as simply existing to fulfil your needs is also going to make intimacy almost impossible. Avoiding the resolution of problems will also cause a breakdown in your relationships.

THE HEALTHY RELATIONSHIP FOR YOU

Being able to handle conflicts and discuss problems with a loved one are the lifeblood of a healthy relationship. Learning to be vulnerable with a lover once the 'honeymoon' period is over could provide closeness in your life. It is now up to you to admit that you may have an intimacy problem, and a vital first step towards this is to be honest with yourself. Learning to come clean means you will have to experience pain and hurt, but it also means finding warmth and closeness with a loved one. So don't be afraid to ask for help from a trained therapist who could enable you to face your pain, and hopefully help you to move on. It's up to you.

8
Love matters.
Who's your perfect type – and who to steer clear of!

Love matters!

A balanced personality type can have healthy relationships with most other types. However, there are some dynamics that send pulses racing, whereas others simply leave the person cold. It's important to remember, though, that sometimes working through the toughest relationship challenges and crises can lead to a fuller and more enriching partnership. Scratch beneath the surface of some relationships, which on the surface seem so easy-going and perfect, and you'll often find deep-rooted problems.

Deep and long-lasting love can occur between two people who appear on the surface to be totally incompatible, so it's clear that there is more to love than some magic formula. By applying the knowledge you've learned about the different personality types we've studied, you can get further along the road to finding out which relationship could work best for you – and as a result make more informed and smart decisions about your future partner.

LOVE MATTERS. WHO'S YOUR PERFECT TYPE?

On the following pages, we'll take a look at the seven personality types we've been studying. Each can be matched with all the types, but we have focused on examples of possible partnerships that appear to have great potential. We also look at how the types would get on if matched with their own type. At the end of the chapter, we'll take a closer look at case studies that illustrate some of the more challenging dynamics, and outline successful problem-solving techniques to handle them.

PERFECTIONIST

How would this high-achieving type fare with a High Flyer, Thrill Seeker or a fellow Perfectionist?

Perfectionist and High Flyer

A Perfectionist could have a wonderful relationship with a High Flyer. They could appeal to the other's drive, ambition and desire to succeed, pushing each other on to be the very best they can. This could be a sizzling relationship as long as both keep each other's needs in mind.

However, they could also become embroiled in power struggles, and may avoid difficulties by burying problems. This could lead to them becoming critical, focusing too much on their own needs and potentially losing sight of the relationship.

Perfectionist and Thrill Seeker

A Perfectionist could have a great adventure with a Thrill Seeker if they allow themselves to. There would certainly be sparks flying in this dynamic, as the Thrill Seeker introduces the normally controlled Perfectionist to new and exciting experiences. Meanwhile, the 'in control' Perfectionist could also teach the Thrill Seeker how to exercise self-control, and make more informed choices.

One downside, however, could arise if the Perfectionist feels out of control and always wants to be the one who 'wears the trousers', while the Thrill Seeker begins to find their adventurous spirit and imagination being stifled.

What about two Perfectionists together?

This could start off really well, with both partners connecting over their desire to be the very best they can. However, their mutual wish to keep things in check and under control, as well as hide their vulnerabilities, may bring out tensions that, if left unresolved, could lead to resentments and petty jealousies.

NATURAL TALENT

How would a Natural Talent handle a Serial Romantic, a High Flyer or their own type?

Natural Talent and Serial Romantic

A Natural Talent could work really well with a Serial Romantic. This dynamic could be a keeper and has the potential to be a long-term relationship, in which both partners are focused on creating a harmonious atmosphere and minimising tensions.

The relationship could suffer, however, if the Natural

LOVE MATTERS. WHO'S YOUR PERFECT TYPE?

Talent becomes negative, anxious or depressed. This may cause the Serial Romantic to panic and flee into the arms of someone else.

Natural Talent and High Flyer

The Natural Talent could also benefit from the attentions of a High Flyer. The High Flyer's positive attitude and gutsy self-belief could rub off on the Natural Talent, and have the wonderful effect of encouraging them to feel better about themselves.

The downside is that, at times, the Natural Talent might feel as though they are being left behind by the aspirationally thirsty High Flyer, and this could lead to increasing self-doubt on the part of the Natural Talent.

What about two Natural Talents together?

This relationship has the potential to succeed if both parties have a sense of their own worth, and a clear understanding of where their vulnerabilities lie. However, if they don't, they could end up becoming stuck in the mud, and outdoing each other in the anxiety-raising stakes.

SERIAL ROMANTIC

How would a Serial Romantic pull out all the stops for a Natural Talent, a Flamboyant Performer or their own type?

Serial Romantic and Natural Talent

Serial Romantics could have a wonderful time with Natural Talents. They may take it upon themselves to ensure that their partner feels loved, and positive about themselves, every minute of the day. And they would not be afraid to leave romantic notes on their pillow, or send flowers. They may go out of their way to provide a loving, stress-free environment, and soothe away the Natural Talent's tendency towards negative thinking.

This dynamic could run into problems, however, if difficulties are simply swept under the carpet and not dealt with, as both these types have a tendency to avoid conflict.

Serial Romantic and Flamboyant Performer
The Serial Romantic could also enjoy an intimate relationship with a Flamboyant Performer. The latter could find an adoring admirer in the Serial Romantic, who would enjoy lavishing attention on them and be prepared to put their partner on a pedestal.

This couple may become unstuck if the Flamboyant Performer starts to feel that attention is drifting from them, however, and wonders if the Serial Romantic is tiring of them. This might cause a rift and leave both wondering if it's time to seek out new experiences.

What about two Serial Romantics together?
These two may have trouble leaving the bedroom, as they seek to out-romance each other. They may be so in love with each other's company that they may be in danger of cutting other relationships out of their lives. This could leave them highly dependent on each other, and in danger of losing their sense of individual identity.

LOVE MATTERS. WHO'S YOUR PERFECT TYPE?

> **THRILL SEEKER**

How would this daredevil type romance a High Flyer, a Perfectionist or a fellow Thrill Seeker?

Thrill Seeker and High Flyer

This has the potential to be an explosive dynamic. These two types would be very attracted to each other, finding appeal in their mutual fearlessness. Their determination makes them instantly compelling to each other. Their sex life has the potential to be one of the most adventurous and exciting. However, problems could occur if the High Flyer feels that they are being led astray by the Thrill Seeker's need for new experiences, and a power struggle may well ensue.

Thrill Seeker and Perfectionist

Possibly one of the most creative partnerships of all. Whereas the Perfectionist may be ordered and controlling, the Thrill Seeker can introduce excitement and the confidence to push boundaries. Although both can learn from each other, the potential to rub each other up the wrong way is never far away, however!

What about two Thrill Seekers together?

Two Thrill Seekers together are instantly attracted to each other. They have the potential to be a most compatible couple, as they recognise a kindred spirit, and form a powerful connection. But they also have the potential to be most destructive together, as they may find it tough to rein each other in or exercise moderation (see later in this chapter for a fuller examination of this personality match).

EXHIBITIONIST

How would this alluring type love a Flamboyant Performer, a High Flyer or their own type?

Exhibitionist and Flamboyant Performer

An Exhibitionist has the potential to have a wonderful time with a Flamboyant Performer if they allow themselves to. The Flamboyant Performer would bring out the star quality of the Exhibitionist, and together they would enjoy painting the town red.

This relationship could suffer, however, if the Exhibitionist feels ignored and neglected by the antics of the Flamboyant Performer, and, in a bid to avoid confrontation, may end the relationship.

Exhibitionist and High Flyer

The Exhibitionist and the High Flyer could potentially have a lot of fun together. They could engage in a game of 'dare', and push each other to new heights. Both would be willing to try out new things – like dropping everything and travelling the world at a moment's notice Their biggest challenge would be how to manage the relationship once the initial buzz of the 'honeymoon period' has died down, and they would need to find a balance, put down boundaries and create the space to deal with problems.

LOVE MATTERS. WHO'S YOUR PERFECT TYPE?

What about two Exhibitionists together?

Two Exhibitionists could possibly make for one of the most contentious dynamics. They may well be attracted to each other's love of the dramatic, but they may also compete for centre stage. This relationship could go either way. They have the potential to become soul mates if they allow closer emotional intimacy, or instead become the 'on again–off again' couple as they continue to hide behind a series of masks.

FLAMBOYANT PERFORMER

How would this larger-than-life type woo a Serial Romantic, an Exhibitionist or their own type?

Flamboyant Performer and Serial Romantic

The Flamboyant Performer would have a great time with a Serial Romantic. The Flamboyant Performer would simply adore the attentions of their lover. These two would probably have the best dinner parties, go on the most romantic holidays and live the most expensive and glamorous lifestyle, and certainly the Flamboyant Performer would thoroughly enjoy the attention that this would bring.

They may come unstuck, however, if the Serial Romantic feels pushed out, and lonely within the relationship. This could bring about tensions and lead to silent stand-offs.

Flamboyant Performer and Exhibitionist

The Flamboyant Performer could have an indulgent time

with an Exhibitionist, perhaps able to live out exciting and daring romantic fantasies. However, once things start to get serious, the power balance between these two types could make or break their relationship. The Exhibitionist may find themselves needing to feel valued, and the Flamboyant Performer may find themselves striving to retain centre stage.

What about two Flamboyant Performers together?
Two Flamboyant Performers together would have a most dramatic and indulgent time. They would enjoy aiming for the same goals – that of being loved and adored for being so fabulous. They may really struggle when it comes to relationship conflicts and rows, though, as both may find it tough to deal with their own vulnerabilities and potentially see it as a personal attack on their egos.

HIGH FLYER

How would this ambitious type seduce a Thrill Seeker, Perfectionist or their own type?

High Flyer and Thrill Seeker
This sexy couple have all the potential to make it, but need to firm up the relationship boundaries and respect each other's need to express their own identity and individuality.

High Flyer and Perfectionist
Both have qualities that the other truly admires. Love

could come unstuck, however, if the High Flyer comes to feel cornered and criticised by the Perfectionist.

What about two High Flyers together?
Two High Flyers in love could have an amazing experience. They would have no trouble understanding each other's ambitious nature, and would be generous enough to encourage their partner to be the very best they can. Their biggest problem could be the potential of losing the sexual spark between them. Why? Because they are in danger of prioritising their work schedule and postponing sex and romance for another day!

MAKING CHALLENGING RELATIONSHIPS WORK

Now that you have looked at the best, let's take a closer look at four examples of potentially challenging dynamics. In each case, we'll examine the relationship and then ask the following questions:

What could they gain from each other?
Where could the flashpoints lie?
How could a more balanced approach work for them?

Perfectionist and Flamboyant Performer
What kind of relationship might a Perfectionist have with a Flamboyant Performer? And could it work?

CELEBRITY LIFE LAUNDRY

CASE STUDY

Jenny is a Perfectionist. She comes from a family where hard work and effort meant the key to future success. She was driven and very capable in her career, rarely making time to sit back and enjoy herself. When it came to relationships, she often found it tricky to maintain intimacy. Her pattern was to choose long-distance relationships, which really suited her, as she could always keep control of when she saw her boyfriends, and it was almost always Jenny who ended the relationship.

Jenny has been with Pete for nine months now, and things are starting to get serious. For Jenny, this is the first time she has allowed herself to get close to someone. She took the unusual step, for her, of deciding to move in with Pete. They have been living together for a few months, and Pete has decided that he wants to get engaged.

Pete is a Flamboyant Performer. He comes from a family where he was one of four children. He often felt that his needs were ignored, and used to have to work extremely hard to impress his parents and his peers. At school, he was the class clown, and became popular and known for it. As an adult, he is the life and soul at parties. He sets pulses racing when he walks into a room.

The good points

Pete has been great for Jenny, in that he has helped to bring her out of her shell. Instead of being so focused on work, Jenny has allowed herself to let her hair down and take a few risks. But, in typical Jenny style, she consulted

LOVE MATTERS. WHO'S YOUR PERFECT TYPE?

her checklist of Pete's good and bad points before considering whether to move in with him.

Since moving in, though, she has been less controlling in the relationship, understanding that she doesn't always have to organise everything. She has even begun to see that, when Pete is late home, it doesn't mean that he doesn't love her any more.

Jenny has been good for Pete, too. He has calmed down a lot, and has realised that he doesn't always need to be centre stage in order to be loved. He has learned to notice when Jenny is feeling low, and has made time to listen to her needs.

The flashpoint
However, Jenny went into a panic when Pete proposed, suddenly feeling stifled, hemmed in and out of control, doubting whether she'd made the right decision to live with him. Pete started to find her behaviour unnerving, but he felt afraid to talk to her. Instead, he started spending more and more time with his mates, going to clubs and flirting outrageously with other women in order to deal with his fears.

Things came to a head when a friend of Jenny's saw Pete canoodling with another girl at a club. They had a huge row, which left them both reeling. Jenny couldn't deal with the betrayal, and Pete blamed her for pushing him away.

What went wrong?
Instead of being open about her fears around making the relationship more permanent, Jenny retreated to her tried-

and-tested way of behaving. She withdrew from Pete, and became distant in order to regain her sense of control.

Pete also reverted to a safe way of behaving. He recognised that Jenny was becoming distant, but felt too frightened to confront his anxieties, fearing that the relationship would be over. He unwittingly sabotaged it all, by taking comfort in the arms of another woman.

Resolving the problem in a balanced way
Jenny and Pete need to learn to recognise their own patterns of thinking.

They both felt vulnerable, but reacted to it in different ways. Jenny withdrew, and Pete simply ran away. Jenny has to recognise that her need for control comes in many forms. Moving in with Pete was fine, but marriage was a situation she felt trapped in. Pete has to face up to his need to flee from confrontation, because it makes him feel helpless.

By recognising what they both do and being honest about it, the two of them have a real chance to recover from this and make it work.

Natural Talent and Exhibitionist
What kind of relationship might a Natural Talent have with an Exhibitionist? And could it work?

CASE STUDY
Fiona is a Natural Talent. She is known for being fantastic at whatever she turns her attention to. As far back as primary school, the teachers loved her, but also

LOVE MATTERS. WHO'S YOUR PERFECT TYPE?

noticed her shyness, and a real determination to down play her abilities.

She is adored and popular at work, and has a close circle of friends. When it comes to relationships, Fiona certainly feels as though she's had her heart broken many times, and has often been dumped by her boyfriends. Her pattern has been to go for guys who love to dominate her. She's been able to handle this by playing a supporting role to their egos.

Fiona has been with Dave for two years, and there have been niggling problems, but on the whole she has felt that, as long as she handles him right, all will be well. Fiona's friends don't really think much of Dave, and couldn't understand how the relationship had lasted this long. Fiona's parents also disliked Dave, but at the same time felt relieved that she'd managed to have a relationship for this long.

Dave is an Exhibitionist. He comes from what he says was a very loving family, although his dad had a drink problem. Dave learned very early on how to keep the family secrets, but at times this has meant that he can't talk about what he has been through because he believes that it will be like betraying his dad. He often bottles up his feelings, choosing instead to act like a jack the lad. He is known as a bit of a show-off, and can often embarrass Fiona when they're out with their friends.

The good points

In Fiona, Dave has found someone who really cares about his feelings, and is truly there for him. He says that she's the only person who knows the real him. He has felt able to take small steps towards opening up about what he went through as a child, which he thinks has enabled both of them to develop a closer bond. At times, though, Jenny has felt as though he keeps her at arm's length when it comes to emotional difficulties

Dave has helped Fiona to feel good about her achievements, and refuses to let her put herself down. Fiona has allowed herself to take small steps to accept that she is a good person, and this has really helped to boost her confidence.

The flashpoint
Dave had started drinking heavily. He found it increasingly difficult to get up for work in the morning and regularly asked Fiona to ring in sick for him. Fiona started finding bottles hidden in the airing cupboard and the bathroom. She became worried, but felt afraid to challenge him about it. They got into a vicious cycle of pretending things were fine; Dave would act sober, and Fiona would collude with this behaviour and lie on his behalf.

What went wrong?
Dave clearly had a drink problem, but was in denial about it. He had swiftly become accustomed to lying and being secretive, as this script from the past was deeply entrenched in him.

Fiona took on the role of enabler and supported Dave's habit, feeling powerless to challenge and confront him about his behaviour. She had an underlying fear that she would lose Dave by confronting him, which would realise her worst fears – that she wasn't good enough to stay with.

Resolving the problem in a balanced way
Fiona and Dave were so caught up in their own negative beliefs about themselves that they weren't able to recognise how they were both affecting the relationship.

Fiona needs to stop being an enabler, which she does by indirectly encouraging Dave to remain secretive. She also has to recognise that her negative belief about herself – that she is never good enough – is affecting how she behaves in this situation. Dave needs help to confront his drinking problem, which he uses as a way to block out difficult emotions.

If Fiona is honest about her feelings, then Dave will have to wake up to his own behaviour. Only then can they break out of this traumatic cycle and move on.

Serial Romantic and High Flyer

What kind of relationship could they have? And could it work?

CASE STUDY

Tim is a Serial Romantic. He was a well-loved little boy at school, creating harmonious friendships, adored by his peers and teachers alike. Tim was brought up in a family dominated by women. His dad left home when he was just a baby and he has no clear memories of him. He is the youngest of five children, and the only boy. He was, and still is, very close to his mum and sisters.

CELEBRITY LIFE LAUNDRY

When it comes to relationships, Tim has no trouble getting girlfriends. He knows how to flatter women and tends to fall in love very quickly. He's had a number of long-term relationships and maintains friendships with all of his exes.

Tim has been dating Bea for about a year, but they don't live together. He fell for her immediately, and has been besotted with her ever since. Their friends see their relationship as perfect, and think that they'll grow old together and have lots of children.

Bea is a High Flyer. Since she was a little girl, she has been very ambitious. Both her parents had high hopes for her, and as an only child she got a lot of attention from both of them. Her mum in particular wanted her to be the best at whatever she did.

In her love life, Bea has had a few long-term relationships, but has often found that the men in her life complained that her ambitions were more important than they were. She found this frustrating, and relationships often ended with her making a late-night call, telling her partner that things just weren't working out.

Bea loves her job. She is a successful interior designer running her own business, and finds her work exhilarating.

The good points
In Bea, Tim has found someone exciting and dynamic, someone who is independent and fearless in trying out new ideas. This has been good for him, as at times he has found it difficult to take up new challenges.

In Tim, Bea has found a stable and attentive boyfriend.

LOVE MATTERS. WHO'S YOUR PERFECT TYPE?

She adores Tim, and finds his company inspiring. She loves bouncing ideas off him, and loves the way he supports her.

The flashpoint
Bea and Tim started to experience problems very gradually. There was no big argument or disagreement, but both started to feel dissatisfied. Bea sometimes complained to her friends that Tim was too clingy, although she loved him dearly. Tim, at times, felt as though he was an appendage to Bea's life. He told one of his sisters that he feared Bea was becoming a workaholic and that she treated him simply as a sounding board, not as an equal partner.

What went wrong?
Both Bea and Tim had dissatisfactions with each other. There weren't major problems, but both felt as though things weren't quite right. Tim started to feel anxious if Bea didn't call when he expected her to. He resorted to leaving her numerous messages at work, and organising elaborate dinner dates to impress her. The more Tim did, the more Bea buried herself in her work. She started avoiding his calls, going out with other friends without telling him and turning up late for dates. Tim was behaving in a clingy and dependent way – something Bea loathed – and Bea became more self-absorbed and distant from Tim – something he feared.

Resolving the problem
Tim had managed to create an atmosphere that realised

his worst fears. His tried-and-tested method of avoiding difficulties was to go all out to smooth things over, and build harmony. He hated being single – it made him feel anxious – so, rather than face up to the reasons he was annoyed with Bea, he buried his true feelings.

Bea avoided Tim by focusing on her work, her own life and independence. She enjoyed her life and, if she was being really honest, she did treat Tim like an accessory, to be picked up and dropped whenever she felt like it.

Tim needs to recognise his own fears about being single. By doing this, he would start to understand and face up to his pattern of clingy behaviour whenever the relationship seems under threat.

Bea needs to recognise that she engages in avoidance behaviour when it comes to her personal life. She employs selfish tactics by being self-absorbed, and putting her own needs first, choosing to ignore her negative behaviour and to blame Tim instead. She needs to appreciate that relationships are about a partnership, where give and take and compromise are key.

A relationship where one person is very independent and the other has dependency issues can be extremely challenging. It can lead to resentments if both people don't recognise their own behaviours and beliefs about relationships.

Tim may feel threatened by Bea's honesty, but it would help him to face up to his fears. Bea needs to hear how her selfish behaviour is hurting her partner, and recognise that until she breaks this pattern she is in danger of alienating her lovers.

LOVE MATTERS. WHO'S YOUR PERFECT TYPE?

What about two Thrill Seekers together?

What kind of relationship could they have together? And could it work?

CASE STUDY

Siobhan is a Thrill Seeker. She is full of energy, buzzing with ideas and has no problem coming up with exciting plans. Unsurprisingly, she has found her way into working in a creative environment – making documentaries in war-torn countries – which truly enables her to get her buzz.

Siobhan was brought up in a lively family of two brothers and two sisters; she was the middle child. Her parents were always on the move, as her father was a diplomat. Siobhan was sent to boarding school at 11, and spent most of the time dreaming up, and carrying out, elaborate ways to escape.

When it comes to romance, Siobhan has often found it tricky to maintain long-term relationships, and certainly has a preference for short bursts of intense and exciting love affairs, which end as dramatically as they started.

Siobhan has only recently started dating Richard. They work together, and their romance of six months has been the talk of the office.

Richard is also a Thrill Seeker. He has been a journalist for ten years, and has travelled to far-flung places in the world. Richard loves his job, and is passionate about it. He came from a family of journalists, and that sense of excitement as a news story broke was the atmosphere he grew up in. As an only child, he showed a keen interest in finding out about other places, and developed a thirst for travel as he got older.

The good points
Siobhan and Richard were working on a news story together, and instantly hit it off. This was the start of an exciting connection.

Since then, their time together has been intense, meaningful and full of ideas and big plans. They both have an understanding of where the other person is coming from. This instant connection has meant that they really feel a deeper emotional connection.

The flashpoints
Although they have an understanding of each other's career, as the relationship has become more meaningful, arguments have also started to break out. Although this is a natural part of new relationships, Richard's habit of taking off at the drop of a hat, and calling Siobhan from abroad to announce that he is covering a story, has left her fuming and believing that he doesn't think much of her, as it seems he can't be bothered to tell her of his trips in advance. Siobhan is not guilt-free either. She can become so absorbed in putting a documentary together that she loses track of time, and has left Richard sitting in a restaurant waiting for hours for her to turn up.

What went wrong?
What has brought these two people together is also what is in danger of pushing them apart. Although they

admire each other's spirit, to some extent they are also angered by it.

Siobhan believes that it is Richard's responsibility to recognise her worth, but is not as self-aware when it comes to how she treats him. Richard, in turn, assumes that Siobhan should understand his ambitions and, no matter how thoughtless he might be, that it is her role to be accepting of it.

Resolving the problem in a balanced way

Siobhan needs to reflect on her own part in the relationship, and recognise her expectations of Richard. In turn, Richard has to challenge his strongly held beliefs that Siobhan's role in the relationship is to accept his behaviour without question.

By understanding the part they each play in the potential breakdown of communication, and in bringing about misunderstandings, the two of them have a real opportunity to recognise and address their own long-held beliefs – and, by doing this, enable the relationship to go to the next level.

9
Resources For a Little Extra Help

There are times when a little extra help can go a long way. If you're in emotional distress for any reason, don't isolate yourself. Pick up the phone and talk about it with a good friend. If you need specific advice, visit your doctor for a confidential chat. And if you need a little extra help with a deep emotional problem, or are in a crisis or suffering from a long-term problem, then there are many excellent organisations who can advise, support and provide the information that'll help you help yourself.

I WANT TO SEE A THERAPIST

If you are thinking of seeing a therapist for the first time, the chances are you might feel a bit nervous. Don't worry, that's an absolutely normal reaction. The best way to start is by doing some research. Contact one of the main counselling professional bodies such as the BACP or BPS included in the list below. They will then send you a list of therapists in your area, with details of their qualifications and professional experience.

RESOURCES FOR A LITTLE EXTRA HELP

Choose a couple of names from the list, and then give the therapist a call who may suggest an initial consultation appointment. This is a great opportunity to decide whether you feel comfortable with the therapist. Even if you do, it is a good idea to visit a couple more therapists before you decide. Remember, you can choose to see a male or female therapist, someone older or younger – whoever you feel at ease with.

Three key points to remember
1. The therapy is for you.
2. Trust your instincts.
3. Ask lots of questions.

What do I ask the therapist?
How long have you been practising as a therapist?
What kind of problems do you cover?
What method of counselling do you use?
Is the therapy open-ended or time-limited?
How much do you charge?

What should I expect?
A good therapist will answer all your questions clearly and realistically. If you feel comfortable and happy to proceed, then the therapist may suggest you have a working contract between the two of you. This will cover things like a confidentiality clause, fees, appointment times, whether the therapy is time-limited or open-ended, etc. If for any reason you don't want to proceed, you can walk away and try someone else.

CELEBRITY LIFE LAUNDRY

What if I'm concerned about how things are going?

If you ever have cause for concern about the therapy or the therapist, and feel unable to talk to them about it, then contact a professional body like the BACP or BPS who will investigate it on your behalf, advise you and take any appropriate action, if necessary.

ORGANISATIONS AND ADDRESSES FOR FURTHER HELP

Alcohol Concern
Waterbridge House
32–36 Loman Street
London
Tel: 020 7928 7377

Advice and information given on alcohol and its effects, with details of UK treatment centres.

British Association for Counselling and Psychotherapy
1 Regent Place
Rugby
Warwickshire
CV21 2PJ
Tel: 0788 578328
www.counselling.co.uk

Professional body for psychotherapists in the UK, providing a comprehensive list of counsellors, also offering advice and information on therapy.

RESOURCES FOR A LITTLE EXTRA HELP

British Association for Behavioural and Cognitive Psychotherapies
PO Box 9
Accrington
Lancashire
BB5 2GD
Tel: 01245 875277
www.babcp.com

Professional body providing a list of therapists, and advice on cognitive behavioural psychotherapies.

British Psychological Society
St Andrews House
48 Princess Road East
Leicester
LE1 7DR
Tel: 01162 549568
www.bps.org.uk

Professional body for psychologists, also offering extra information and details of psychologists.

CRUSE Bereavement Care
Cruse House
126 Sheen Road
Richmond
Surrey, TW9 1UR
Tel: 020 8944818
www.crusebereavementcare.org.uk

CELEBRITY LIFE LAUNDRY

Information advice and support for those who have been bereaved, with details of local UK branches.

Drink Line (The National Alcohol Helpline)
Petersham House
57 Hatton Garden
London EC1N 8HP
Tel: 0345 320202

Information and advice for those with alcohol-related problems.

MIND
Granta House
15–19 Broadway
Stratford
London
E15 4BQ
Tel: 020 8512122
www.mind.org.uk
Information line: 08457 660163

RESOURCES FOR A LITTLE EXTRA HELP

Information and advice on a wide range of mental health problems.

National Phobic Society
Zion Community Resource Centre
339 Stretton Road
Hulme
Manchester
M15 4ZY
Tel: 0870 770 0456
www.phobics-society.org.uk

The largest charity dealing with anxiety and disorders, providing information, advice and support. Run by sufferers and ex-sufferers of anxiety disorders.

No Panic
93 Brands Farm Way
Telford
Shropshire
TF3 2JQ
Helpline: 01952 590545
Tel: 01952 590005
www.no-panic.co.uk

CELEBRITY LIFE LAUNDRY

Help for those suffering with panic attacks, phobias and obsessive/compulsive disorder.

OCD-UK
PO Box 8115
Nottingham
NG7 1YT
www.admin@ocduk.org

Leading UK charity for people who are affected by obsessive/compulsive disorder. Run by sufferers and ex-sufferers. Provides information, advice and support.

Relate
Herbert Gray College
Little Church Street
Rugby
Warwickshire
CV21 3AP
Tel: 0870 6012121
www.relate.org.uk

Information and counselling for couples.

Bibliography

Adderholt-Eliot, M., 'Perfectionism and Underachievement', in *Gifted Child Today* 12(1), 1989, pp19–21.

Alvear, Q? IS THIS Michael?, 'Risky Business', www.salon.com, 1999.

Barrow, J. C., & Moore, C. A., 'Group Interventions with Perfectionist Thinking', in *Personnel and Guidance Journal* 61, 1983, pp612–615.

Baruch, G. K., 'Girls who Perceive themselves as Competent: Some Antecedents and Correlates' in *Psychology of Women* 1, 1976, pp38–49.

Beck, Aaron T.; Freeman, Arthur; Davies, Denise, D., and associates, *Cognitive Therapy of Personality Disorders*, second edition, New York: Guilford Press, 2003.

Bornstein, Robert F., *The Dependent Personality*, New York: Guilford Press, 1993.

Flett, Gordon L., 'York University Researcher Finds that Perfectionism Can Lead to Imperfect Health', in *Media Release Archive*, 2004, www.yorku.ca/mediar/archive/release

Goleman, D., *Emotional Intelligence*, Bloomsbury, 1996.

BIBLIOGRAPHY

Jackson, Melissa, 'Why Perfect is not always Best', www.bbc.co.uk/1/hi/health/3815479.stm

Kizziar, Janet, 'Counselling Survivors of Dysfunctional Families', class presented at the University of California, Riverside, 21 January 1989.

Llewellyn, Dr J., risktaking.co.uk.

McClelland, D., *Human Motivation*, Cambridge University Press, 1988.

Mchale, S., & Hunt, N., 'Thrill seekers find life is sweeter', Nottingham Trent University and Sheffield Hallam University, 2002.

Milloy, J. Steven, 'Thrill Seeking Gene Found', www.junkscience.com/news2/thrill.htm.

Namka, Lynne (ed), 'Selfishness and narcissism in family relationships', www.angriesout.com, 2005.

Namka, Lynne, 'The doormat syndrome, www.angriesout.com, 1989.

Namka, Lynne, 'Talk, trust and feel therapeutics', www.angriesout.com, 2002.

Silverman, L. K., 'Perfectionism', paper presented at the 11th World Conference on Gifted and Talented Children, Hong Kong, 1995.

Trubo, Richard, 'Thrill seekers thrive on the scary', for quotes from Frank Farley. www.webm.d.co/content/article/53/50452.htm.

Weiner, Bernard, *Human Motivation*, Holt, Rinehart and Winston, 1980.

Zuckerman, M., *Behavioural Expression and Biosocial Bases of Sensation Seeking*, Cambridge University Press, 1994.